TIPI RINGS

TIPI RINGS

A CHRONICLE OF THE JICARILLA APACHE LAND CLAIM

ROBERT J. NORDHAUS

BOWARROW PUBLISHING COMPANY
ALBUQUERQUE

Manufactured in the United States of America

Typesetting by Databased Imaging Systems, Inc.

Library of Congress Catalog Card Number: 94-78671

ISBN 1-885931-00-X

To Dick Davis,
who introduced me to the field of Indian Law

and

To the Jicarilla Apache Tribe,
without whose support and vision of the future
none of this story would have come to pass

Robert J. Nordhaus

A native New Mexican, Robert J. Nordhaus was born in Las Vegas, New Mexico, in 1909. After graduating from Albuquerque High School in 1927 he attended Yale College and earned his law degree from the Yale Law School in 1935. He returned to Albuquerque, where he established his residence and has lived ever since. There he practiced law until his retirement in 1987, except for five years of service as an officer in the United States Army. During World War II he served in Italy with the famed 10th Mountain Division.

As the result of a meeting arranged by his college friend, Denver lawyer Richard M. Davis, with Roy Mobley, the general counsel for the Tribe, Mobley persuaded Davis and Nordhaus to help him prosecute a land claim of the Jicarilla Apache Tribe against the United States. After the successful conclusion of that claim in 1971, the law firm, then known as Nordhaus, Moses, and Dunn, became general counsel for the Jicarilla Apache Tribe. Since 1970 Mr. Nordhaus has specialized in Indian law, and the firm (since split from the Moses firm) now known as Nordhaus, Haltom, Taylor, Taradash and Frye has become one of the most prominent Indian law firms in the United States.

Mr. Nordhaus is recognized as the "founder" of the La Madera Ski Area (now Sandia Peak), which came into service in 1937, and was instrumental in the development and construction of the Sandia Peak Tramway in 1964. He has been engaged in ranching and real-estate development. An avid sportsman, he took up flying his own plane when he received his pilot's license at age 59. Now, at age 85, he continues to be an active and enthusiastic skier, tennis player, and fly fisherman . . .

CONTENTS

• • •

ILLUSTRATIONS

• • •

MAPS

PLATES

CHARTS

PREFACE

• • •

Tipi rings—circles of stone left in the vast lands where the Jicarilla Apache buffalo hunters erected their conical tents of hide—disclosed more than 80 campsites and villages located within an area encompassing more than 72,000 square miles of our southwestern United States. For more than three hundred years these sites were regularly used and occupied by the Tribe during their semiannual or annual hunts, until these lands were engulfed by the swell of western migration. Tipi (tepee) rings were to become one of the most compelling items of evidence to be brought forth by the Jicarilla Apache Tribe in its claim for compensation for lands taken by the United States in the 1800s.

My association with the Jicarilla Apache Tribe began with a telephone call from Roy Mobley, who was the general counsel for the Tribe at that time, asking if Richard M. (Dick) Davis and I would be interested in working with him on the Jicarilla Apache land claim that was pending before the Indian Claims Commission.

A few weeks before, Davis, who was a classmate of mine in college, had called me to ask if I would get in touch with Mobley to see if the Tribe would be interested in depositing some of its funds in a bank in Denver represented by his law firm. As a result we met with Mobley and talked for several hours one afternoon at his home; he advised us that he would suggest to the Tribe that it not deposit any funds outside of New Mexico. Davis and I presumed this would be the end of our conversations on the matters of the Tribe.

Some time later Mobley contacted me on the phone to say that he was having trouble handling the Jicarilla Apache Tribe land claim by himself. He said that the Washington attorneys associated with him, Guy Martin and James L. Kunen, had not assisted him on the research involved in the claim, and since Davis and I seemed to have taken an interest in the Tribe, he asked us to become associated with him.

Davis and I talked on the phone and met several times. We studied Indian claims procedures and talked to attorneys in Washington who had worked on Indian claims. We recognized that these claims took a number of years to resolve, required a great deal of work and research, and that they were contingent in nature; one big consideration was that we would have to pay our own expenses. After taking all of this into account, we nevertheless decided that it would be challenging, and agreed to handle the claim.

ACKNOWLEDGMENTS

• • •

Among the many people who assisted in the successful prosecution of the Jicarilla Apache land claim, I wish particularly to mention those whose help was indispensable, as well as others to whom I am greatly indebted.

First I would like to thank the Claims Committee of the Tribe—Lindo Vigil, chairman; Alfred Velarde, secretary; and Calvin Vigil, Severo Caramillo, Henry L. Vicente, and Norman Tecube.

I am also grateful to Chairman J. D. Garcia, Presidents Charlie Vigil and Hubert Velarde, and the various members of the Tribal Council in office during the proceedings who were always ready to help the attorneys and our expert witnesses.

The Tribe's expert witnesses were outstanding. Particularly indispensable was Dr. Frank Hibben, whose testimony, based on his knowledge of the early history of the Tribe's ancestors (the extent of their hunting grounds, the location of their early campsites, their sacred places, the trails they traveled year after year to hunting grounds throughout the claim area), was unchallenged and vital to the success of the claim.

The testimony of Dr. Alfred B. Thomas, an authority on the history of the Spanish period in New Mexico history, was also vitally important. The expert testimonies of Dr. Donald Cutter, historian, Dr. Victor Westphal, historian, and Dr. Leroy Gordon, geographer, were all invaluable. Finally the appraisal of the claim award area made by Mr. Alan McMullen was accepted in great part by the Indian Claims Commission in its findings of fact and opinion on valuation of the award area.

There were numerous attorneys associated with me during the proceedings. Guy Martin of Washington, D.C., was the original attorney of record. James L. Kunen, one of his partners, worked with us on the case. Roy Mobley was the Tribe's general counsel when we were first hired by the Tribe; he was responsible for much of the early research in the case. Members of the Denver law firm of Graham, Davis and Stubbs, and particularly Richard M. (Dick) Davis and Robert H. (Bob) Harry, all worked closely with me throughout the conduct of the hearings and in the writing of briefs. Their help was indispensable. I also am grateful to my law partner at the time, Donald B. Moses, who was patient while I spent many hours on this case.

I also want to recognize Barbara Scales and Karen L. P. Contri, who assisted me in the preparation of my manuscript; Jerry Livingston for his maps; and William C. Finney, David R. Margolin, and Veronica E. Tiller, for their efforts in the editing and preparation of this book. Their assistance was invaluable in making it all come together.

A special thank-you goes to my wife, Marjorie E. Nordhaus, for cheering me on and sustaining me during the two years of work that I put into this project.

PART I

• • •

INTRODUCTION

1

INDIAN LAND CLAIMS

To understand the history of Indian land claims in America and the Indian Claims Commission, it will be helpful to go back to the early days of the settlement of North America by Europeans, the history of the founding of the Republic, and some of the first decisions of the United States Supreme Court.[1]

Indian policy in the United States developed from legal precedents established by European colonists in their relations with Native Americans. The European nations established sovereignty in newly discovered lands by a symbolic act, whereby representatives of the sovereign took possession and claimed exclusive jurisdiction over the discovered lands for that personage (64 Tr. 360–61).

Principles of Spanish jurisprudence found their way into early American Indian law. Legal principles governing Spain's administration of its colonies in the New World were first developed by the Council of the Indies, established by the Spanish king in 1511.

In the sixteenth century, there were contemporary statements as to the rights of Indians in the conquered lands; particulary important was that of the Jesuit theologian Francisco de Vitoria, who was asked by Charles V to comment upon the rights of aborigines in the conquered areas. In 1532 he stated that since the Indians were the true owners of the lands, discovery could convey no title, for discovery can be justified only where property is ownerless, nor could title be claimed upon divine rights of the emperor or the pope, or in the absence of a just war; only voluntary consent of the aborigines would justify annexation of this territory.

The Recopilación

The *Recopilación de Leyes de los Reynos de las Indias* was an official codification of Spanish law that brought together all previous decrees affecting the Indies. It was generally applied throughout Spanish North America, including New Mexico.

One major component of the *Recopilación* was laws for the protection of Indians. For example the discoverers were enjoined from engaging in wars with the Indians or doing them any damage or taking their trade or property. The laws ordered that distribution of lands be made without harm to the Indians, that lands not be given out in prejudice to the Indians, that those lands already confiscated be returned to their owners, and that the Indians be allowed their own lands.

The doctrine of Francisco de Vitoria and others, based on Indian rights of possession, became the foundation of Spanish law in America and subsequently the basis for American law relating to Indian rights to their lands (Felix S. Cohen, *Handbook of Federal Indian Law*, p. 52).

Purchase of Land from the Indians

The American colonies recognized at an early date that it was necessary for their own protection to deal fairly with the Indians and that to accomplish this and to prevent fraud and unfair dealings, government authority to purchase land from the Indians should be required. By 1770 ten of the colonies prohibited the purchase of land from Indians without government authorization.

The Continental Congress pledged itself to secure the friendship of the Indians; to effect this purpose, the Congress in 1784 appointed commissioners authorized to negotiate boundaries and conclude a peace for each tribe. Treaties were entered into with the hostile tribes of the six nations (1784); the Wyandotte, Delaware, Chippewa, and Ottawa Indians (1785); and the St. Stanwich, Fort M'Intosh, and Shawnees (1786). As a result of these treaties, boundaries were established between the United States and the tribes.

In the Hopewell Treaty with the Cherokees in 1785, concluded by other commissions appointed by the Continental Congress, no land was ceded; it was merely a treaty of peace. During the nineteenth century, the United States purchased nearly 95 percent of its public domain for approximately $800 million through treaties of agreement with Indian tribes.

These treaties were evidence of the recognition of Indian title. This did not necessarily mean, however, that the terms of the treaties were carried out. The process, according to one historian, was to invade their lands, confiscate their resources, propose treaties, and then after offering to pay a desperate people for their ceded property, to withhold promised funds by one pretext or another (John Uptown Terrell, *Land Grab*, pp. 27–28).

The United States acquired some 443 million acres between 1789 and 1840 in return for some 31.3 million acres set aside for Indian settlement farther west (H. R. Rosenthal, *Their Day in Court*). On May 28, 1830, the Indian Removal Act was passed by Congress, authorizing President Andrew Jackson to exchange United States territory west of the Mississippi for eastern tribal lands. Tribes were advised that a refusal to emigrate would mean the end of federal protection and would subject them to state jurisdiction.

Although the act provided for the voluntary removal of tribes, military force was threatened or used if necessary. For example, the removal of the Cherokees in 1838 was a forced migration, and more than four thousand Cherokees perished during the trek west in what has become known as "The Trail of Tears."

Tribes of the West

At the conclusion of the Mexican War with the United States, the Treaty of Guadalupe Hildago was signed in 1848.

Articles VIII and IX of the treaty dealt with the property rights of individuals. These articles are as follows:

> **Article VIII.** Mexicans now established in territories previously belonging to Mexico and which remain for the future within the limits of the United States as defined by the present treaty shall be free to continue where they now reside or to remove at any time to the Mexican Republic retaining the property which they possess in the said territories or disposing thereof and removing the proceeds wherever they please without their being subjected on this account to any contribution, tax or charge whatever.
>
> Those who shall prefer to remain in the said territories, may either retain the title and rights of Mexican citizens, or acquire those of citizens of the United States. But they shall be under the obligation to make their election within one year from the date of the exchange of ratifications of this treaty; and those who shall remain in the said territories after the expiration of that year, without having declared their intention to retain the character of Mexicans, shall be considered to have elected to become citizens of the United States.
>
> In the said territories, property of every kind, now belonging to Mexicans not established there, shall be inviolably respected. The present owners, the heirs of these, and all Mexicans who may hereafter acquire said property by contract, shall enjoy with respect to it guaranties equally ample as if the same belonged to citizens [of the U.S.].
>
> **Article IX.** Mexicans who, in the territories aforesaid, shall not preserve the character of citizens of the Mexican republic, conformably with what is stipulated in the preceding article, shall be incorporated into the Union of the United States, and be admitted at the proper time (to be judged of by the Congress of the United States) to the enjoyment of all the rights of citizens of the United States according to the principles of the constitution; and in the meantime shall be maintained and protected in the free enjoyment of their liberty and property, and secured in the free exercise of their religion without restriction.

The Treaty of Guadalupe Hidalgo (95 Stat. 922) thus guaranteed the property rights and citizenship of Indians within the territory, as those rights had been recognized by the Mexican government. When Mexico gained independence from Spain in 1821, a revolutionary pronouncement of Augustín Iturbide of February 24, 1821, known as the Plan of Iguala (which became a fixed principle of Mexican law), elevated the social status of the Indians, who had done much to assure victory in the revolution against Spain. The plan provided in part that all of the inhabitants of New Spain, without distinction, whether of European, African, or Indian descent, were citizens of Mexico with the right to be employed in any post according to their merits and virtues, and that the person and property of all persons (Indians included) were to be respected and protected by the government.

Under the terms of the 1848 treaty, all Indians in New Mexico, whether Pueblo or Apache or Navajo, were guaranteed all the rights of citizens of the United States. Most provisions of the treaty were actually recognized with respect to the Pueblos, but not for the Navajos or Apaches. In 1852 the Apaches in New Mexico signed a treaty at Santa Fe, promising perpetual peace with the United States and the cessation of warlike excursions in New Mexico (10 Stat. 979). No land cessions were included. This was the only treaty with the Apaches ever confirmed by the Senate, although several others were negotiated.

Indians in the Courts

With few exceptions, Indians were denied access to the courts to redress their grievances until the Indian Claims Commission Act of 1946. In *Cherokee Nation v. Georgia,* 30 U.S. (5 Pet.) 1 (1831), an action by the Cherokee Nation to restrain the state of Georgia and its officials from enforcing its laws within the Cherokee territory, the Supreme Court held that the Cherokee Nation was not a foreign nation and that therefore the Court had no original jurisdiction. For the next 115 years, until

1946, Indians generally had no access to the courts to redress grievances or to secure compensation for lands taken from them by conquest or bargained away unfairly through fraudulent treaties, agreements, or executive orders.

Prior to 1855 no citizen could bring an action against the United States on claims for a money judgment; the only recourse was to petition Congress. In 1855 an act was passed establishing the Court of Claims. Its purpose was to decide claims based on statutes, treaties, or the breach of government contracts (treaties were included within the scope of the act). Some tribes filed claims under the 1855 law, but in 1863 Congress amended the law to deny relief to Indians on claims based on treaties (Act of March 3, 1863, 12 Stat. 765, 767). From 1863 to 1881, the federal courts were again effectively closed to Indians.

The Fourteenth Amendment to the Constitution of the United States (1868) declared that all persons born or naturalized in the United States were citizens; presumably Indians were included. However, in *Elk v. Wilkins,* 112 U.S. 94 (1884), the Supreme Court held that Indians were not citizens. Indians in general were thus denied access to the Court of Claims and had to rely on special acts of Congress to secure relief for any claims based on loss of their lands or other injuries.

Although some early treaties granted citizenship options to Indians, and several tribes were granted citizenship by statute, the general effect of these decisions was to make tribal membership and U.S. citizenship almost mutually exclusive. There were certain exceptions—Indians who served in the military during World War I, for example, were granted U.S. citizenship. The Indian Citizenship Act of 1924 finally granted citizenship to all Indians within the territorial limits of the United States; neither rights to tribal property nor tribal membership were impaired (43 Stat. 253, Chap. 233).

In the three years following the granting of citizenship, thirty-seven Indian claims cases were filed in the Court of Claims, in contrast to thirty-nine in the forty years preceding citizenship. The objective of prompt and fair adjudication of Indian claims, however, was not fulfilled. The allowance of large offsets for gratuities (expenditures on behalf of Indians not required by treaty or agreement), for instance, resulted in greatly reduced awards. In sixteen cases involving claims of over $346 million, the Court awarded $13.6 million, but then awarded the government $11 million in offsets, leaving net recoveries of only $2.4 million. "Gratuities" were construed to include government salaries and expenses, the repair of agency buildings, teachers' salaries, and other items. An act was passed in 1935 expressly requiring the Court of Claims to consider offset sums expended gratuitously by the United States for the benefit of tribes or bands (49 Stat. 571, 592, August 12, 1935). The result of this statute was to reduce further the amount of claims awarded to tribes.

The Indian Claims Commission

The Court of Claims had attempted to deal with Indian claims for sixty-five years, but had generally failed in its efforts. Even after 1924, when Indians attained citizenship and access to the Court of Claims was guaranteed, the Court of Claims failed to deal adequately with the problem. This led to a growing movement to expedite matters by establishing an exclusive procedure designed to handle Indian claims, which would redress both legal and moral wrongs, finalize such claims, and settle land titles.

But delay continued to prevail. On December 30, 1930, of the eighty-six cases pending since 1919, only fifteen had been decided (Rosenthal, *Their Day in Court*, p. 55).

During the 1930s three bills were introduced in Congress calling for an Indian Claims Court; five bills were introduced in Congress between 1930 and 1935 advocating an Indian Claims Commission, a fact-finding body with the power only to recommend relief to Congress.

Finally on October 5, 1945, a bill was introduced in the House of Representatives proposing to establish an Indian

Claims Commission that would embody many of the provisions favorable to the Indian claims that had been debated for fifteen years. This bill was passed by Congress and became law when it was signed by President Harry S. Truman on August 13, 1946 (60 Stat. 1049, Chap. 959). The act allowed any identifiable group of Indian claimants residing in the United States or Alaska to sue the government for:

1. Claims in law or equity arising under the Constitution, laws, treaties of the United States, and executive orders of the president.
2. All other claims in law or equity, including those sounding in tort, with respect to which the claimant would have been entitled to sue in a court of the United States if the United States was subject to suit.
3. Claims that would result if the treaties, contracts, and agreements between the claimant and the United States were revised on the grounds of fraud, duress, unconscionable consideration, mutual or unilateral mistake, whether of law or fact, or any other ground cognizable by a court of equity.
4. Claims arising from the taking by the United States, whether as the result of treaty of cession or otherwise, of lands owned or occupied by the claimant without the payment for such lands of compensation agreed to by the claimant.
5. Claims based upon fair and honorable dealings that were not recognized by any existing rule of law or equity.

Parts 3 and 4 allowed Indians new bases for recovery, permitting the Commission to treat Indian treaties as if revised, and gave cognizance to and permitted recovery on moral claims.

What particularly interested the Jicarilla Apache Tribe was a provision that permitted tribes to pursue claims based on aboriginal title. Of importance to the government, and of great concern to all tribes, was a provision that permitted the Commission to set off against the award funds spent by the government gratuitously for the benefit of the claimant—that is, funds spent on behalf of a tribe not required by law and not for the benefit of the government. Not included in gratuitous expenditures were administrative expenses of the government; expenditures for educational, health, or highway purposes; and other similar government expenditures.

In the early years of the Commission's existence, the four-stage procedure for hearing its land cases began with title (whether treaty title or title by use and occupancy from time immemorial). After the claim area was established, either pursuant to a treaty or by proof of aboriginal title, the next step was the determination of the date the land was taken from a tribe. The third stage was valuation of the land as of the date it was taken from a tribe. The last stage of the proceeding was the determination of offsets that might be deducted from the award.

Early Decisions of the Commission

The Commission had to decide at an early date what tribes or groups could file suit. Section II of the act stated that the Commission should hear claims "on behalf of any tribe, band, or other identifiable group of American Indians residing within the territorial limits of the United States or Alaska."

The Commission held early on that this definition included only claims of the 176 groups recognized by the Bureau of Indian Affairs *(Report of the Indian Claims Commission, Sept. 30, 1978,* p. 10*)*. The Jicarilla Apache Tribe, being an Indian Reorganization Act tribe and thus recognized, qualified without question.

The most difficult question was that of defining the territory occupied by nontreaty Indians such as the Jicarilla Apache Tribe. In the case of this tribe, there were early bands whose descendants later became members of the recognized tribe; it was necessary to identify these early bands, to establish that they later became one tribe, and to show that these bands occupied and used the claim area exclusively of other tribes from "time immemorial." Otherwise there could be no compensable interest. If the government established that other competing tribes used the land extensively over a period of years, exclusive use could not be proved.

The Supreme Court of the United States, in *United States v. Santa Fe Pacific R.R. Co.*, 314 U.S. 339 (1941), had stated that exclusive use and occupancy had to apply to a definable territory occupied by a single tribe or its ancestors, in order to establish aboriginal possession. This was the rule followed by the Commission; it sounded simple, but it was not easy to prove.

Prior to the Indian Claims Commission Act, claims based on Indian title (exclusive use and occupancy) were not recognized. The Supreme Court had ruled in *Tee-Hit-Ton Indians v. U.S.*, 348 U.S. 272 (1955), that Indian lands were held by grace of the sovereign and that such interest could be terminated without a constitutional right of compensation. The Court indicated, however, that its decision in the case would not necessarily affect claims under the Indian Claims Commission Act. In the same year, the Court of Claims upheld the Commission's decision, in *Otoe and Missouria Tribe of Indians v. U.S.*, 131 Ct. Claims 593 (1955), that Indian title based on exclusive use and occupancy was compensable under section 2 of the act.

Early bands of Jicarilla Apaches and bands of other hunting tribes generally used certain territories year after year; not continually as did the Pueblos, but seasonally, as required by available food. The Commission had to exercise great latitude in its judgment, based upon anthropological, archaeological, and historical data—sometimes going back more than two hundred years—in deciding whether or not use was "exclusive" and from "time immemorial."

The testimony of experts was critical in proving the facts required at each stage of the proceedings. In the case of the Jicarilla Apache Tribe, experts were selected by the attorneys, with their fees and expenses paid for by the Tribe. If tribes had no resources, however, the act provided that the federal government could pay for the experts.

None of the evidence was "first-hand knowledge." Exclusive use from "time immemorial," "date of taking," and "valuation" all had to be decided based on the interpretation by the experts of historical documents, archaeological findings, early maps, and statements of the Jicarilla elders. Most of the statements of older Indians were taken by deposition.

While testimony before the Commission was primarily that of experts, some of the evidence would not generally be admissible in a court of law. The Commission, however, was generous in admitting hearsay evidence and the statements of experts, because they were the best evidence available.

The hearings were adversary proceedings. Although the government had to make available to the Commission (and to the tribes) needed documents from the archives and records of government departments, it was the task of the attorneys for a tribe to collect this material and make it available to the experts (excepting materials already known to them). The government's own attorneys defended it against the claim, and in the case of the Jicarilla Apaches, the defense was vigorous (and sometimes frivolous and unfair, in the view of the attorneys for the Tribe).

Given such a background, the Jicarilla Apache Tribe's pursuit of its ancestral lands was anything but straightforward.

2

• • •

PRELIMINARY INVESTIGATION AND FIRST HEARINGS

After discussions with Roy Mobley and a review of the material he had collected, we made a preliminary determination that in early times, the ancestors of the Jicarilla Apache Tribe had hunted buffalo throughout most of northeastern New Mexico during the period of buffalo migration in the spring and fall (see map 1).

It also appeared that the Tribe had stayed during the winter months between Taos and Pecos hunting small game, and that much later, tribal members had been placed on a reservation in northwestern New Mexico, with headquarters in Dulce on the Navajo River. At the time of the hearing they were an Indian Reorganization Act tribe with a tribal government, constitution, and law-and-order code, governed by a president, a vice-president, and a tribal council of eight members elected by vote of tribal members. Their president was elected for a four-year term, and the tribal council members were elected for staggered two-year terms (these policies remain unchanged today).

We also learned that in order to prosecute the claim, we had to have a claims contract approved by the Tribe and the Bureau of Indian Affairs.

We were introduced to the Tribal Council by Mobley, at a meeting in Dulce, New Mexico. Neither Dick Davis nor I had had any experience with Indian law, nor had we previously had any Indian clients. Nevertheless the Tribal Council and the Bureau of Indian Affairs approved the contract.

Establishing proof would be difficult, because we were interested in the time period between one and three hundred years ago. For some of that time there were written records; during other periods there were none. The Spanish had maintained detailed records of the activities of their governors of New Mexico until 1821, the date of the Mexican revolution. Spanish authorities cited numerous contacts with Apache bands, ancestors of the present-day Jicarilla Apaches.

Mexican authorities maintained practically no records, however. There was no written history of the Apaches for the period from 1821 to 1846, the date of the American occupation. After that date there were many documents recording contacts of the early governors of New Mexico and military commanders with the Jicarilla Apache Tribe and other Indians.

Roy Mobley had contracted with the Stanford Research Institute to investigate the American documents for the period from 1848 to 1887, the date the Jicarilla Apache Tribe was permanently placed on its present reservation. Those documents comprised ten volumes, which were delivered to us in time to be presented at the first hearing date before the Commission in December 1958. In addition to this historical evidence, it was necessary to obtain anthropological and archaeological evidence to establish the extent of the hunting grounds of the Jicarilla Apaches and to determine whether these hunting grounds were used by them exclusively of other tribes.

It was also necessary to establish that the early bands, described variously by the Spaniards, were the same Indians as those who later became the organized Jicarilla Apache Tribe. Dr. Frank C. Hibben, a professor of anthropology at the University of New Mexico, was hired as our expert witness with respect to the archaeology and anthropology of the Apaches.

Dr. Hibben was eminently qualified, having studied the anthropology and archaeology of various Apache tribes and other ancient civilizations in the Southwest. He was also a big-game hunter and had written several books on big-game hunting in North America. We were particularly fortunate in selecting Dr. Hibben, because in 1933, when he had graduated

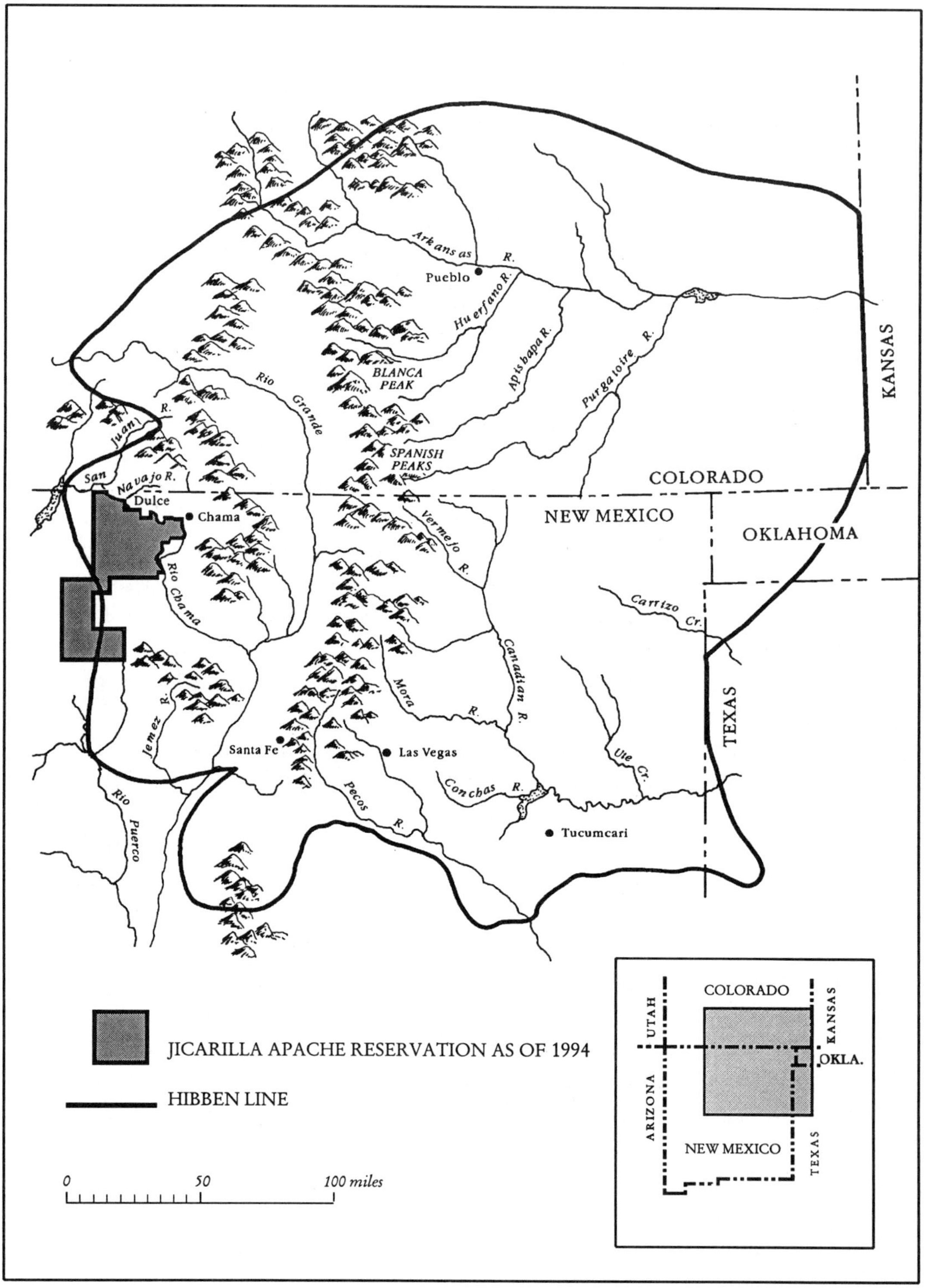

Map 1
Jicarilla Apache Reservation as of 1994

from college and before he went to graduate school, he spent six months in New Mexico hunting wild horses with a man named McDonald. With them on these hunting trips was an Indian named Juan Dedios, who was ninety years old in 1933. He was born a Navajo, was captured by the Spaniards, and escaped and married a Jicarilla Apache. Prior to the Civil War and afterwards, he traveled with Jicarilla Apache bands on many of their hunting trips.

During the six months Dr. Hibben spent with Juan Dedios, he visited Jicarilla Apache hunting camps over the entire claim area in New Mexico and Colorado. He took field notes of all hunting camps located by Juan Dedios and made drawings of camp sites, describing the artifacts found in each camp, such as stone tools, arrowheads, pottery, and cartridges.

In the summer of 1958, I spent several months with Dr. Hibben revisiting these hunting sites. He rechecked his earlier field notes. We took slides and photographs of many of these campsites and of the artifacts we found. These were presented in evidence, and many of them are included in this account.

Dr. Alfred B. Thomas, professor of history at the University of Alabama and an authority on the Spanish history of New Mexico, was employed as the historical expert for the Tribe. Dr. Thomas had written several books, including *After Coronado* (a record of Spanish explorations in New Mexico from the early 1700s to the end of the century), *Spanish Explorations Northeast of New Mexico, Forgotten Frontiers,* and *Plains Indians of New Mexico*, as well as other publications.

Dr. Thomas wrote a report presented in evidence, establishing that the Spaniards had many contacts with the Jicarilla Apache bands and that after 1776 these bands had been allied with the Spaniards and had accompanied the Spanish expeditions from Santa Fe up to the northeast to establish the extent of French penetration into Kansas and to the west. This report showed that Jicarilla Apache bands were familiar with the territory north and east of Santa Fe in the claim area and beyond.

Robert H. (Bob) Harry, a senior partner of Davis, Graham & Stubbs, worked with Dr. Thomas, questioned him before the Commission, and continued to work with me throughout the case.

The Stanford Research Report

The Stanford Research Report contained ten volumes. Eight were reprints of reports of governors of New Mexico, Indian agents, and military personnel, which contained many references to contacts with the Apaches. Volumes 1 and 2 were narratives of historians of such doubtful credentials that we elected not to offer them in evidence.

At the hearing in December, 1958, we offered volumes 3 through 10 in evidence. The government objected on the basis that the complete report was not offered, so we were obliged to submit volumes 1 and 2 over our objection. However, in spite of the fact that these volumes were admitted, I believe that our objections (and the evidence contained in the deposition that the authors were not really qualified) were all important in the evaluation of the evidence by the Commission.

Treaties

It was essential to determine whether treaties had been entered into between the Jicarilla Apaches (the ancestors of the Jicarilla Apache Tribe) and the government of the United States after United States occupation of the territory. It was important to establish whether these treaties had set forth a reservation for the Tribe and whether that reservation comprised all of the lands claimed by the Tribe. If the lands had been taken, it would also be necessary to determine whether the compensation given to the Tribe for those lands was adequate.

General Kearny occupied New Mexico in 1846. The Treaty of Guadalupe Hidalgo was signed between the United States and Mexico in February 1848 (the importance of this treaty is explained in greater detail in Part II). Territorial governors and

Indian agents were ordered to defend the inhabitants against Indian excursions, all of which were blamed on the Apaches. These (U.S.) officials were instructed to negotiate treaties with the Apaches in New Mexico.

No treaty of cession between the United States and the Jicarilla Apaches, nor any agreement or contract to purchase, ever became operative, although several were negotiated (Commission Finding number 3, entered August 26, 1963). It was established that the Apaches were not removed from or deprived of their lands (their lands were not taken by the United States) until they were placed on the reservation.

As we will show later, the Jicarilla Apaches continued to hunt and engage in their normal activities in the claim area until they were finally placed on their permanent reservation in 1887.

The Hearings

Hearings were held in Washington on the question of liability of the United States to the Tribe, the first stage of the proceedings, beginning December 1, 1958. Our opening statement is worth summarizing, as it sets forth the general outlines of the claim and the defenses of the government. We stated that the original claim was filed in February 1948 on behalf of the Apache Nation; that it was amended in October 1950; and that in January 1958 the Jicarilla Apache Claim was separated from other Apache claims as docket number 22.

We explained to the Commission in our introduction that the government had advanced a number of technical defenses that we considered insubstantial. The government denied that the Tribe could legally have ancestors and denied that it was a tribe of American Indians residing in the United States, possessing a tribal organization recognized by the secretary of the interior as having authority to represent an act of the Tribe. This was ludicrous, as the government attorneys knew that the Tribe was an Indian Reorganization Act (IRA) tribe with a constitution approved by the secretary of the interior and a tribal council authorized to act for the Tribe.

The Indian Reorganization Act of 1934, 48 Stat. 984, Chap. 576 (June 18, 1934), was designed to encourage the economic development and self-determination of tribes. It gave tribes authorization to adopt a constitution, which in turn provided a congressional sanction for self-government. The constitution vested in "such Tribe or its Council," among other things, the right to employ counsel subject to the approval of the secretary of the interior. Such attorneys had the authority under the Indian Claims Commission Act to represent a tribe in claims brought before that body.

The government then objected to the admission of the printed charter and constitution of the Tribe and demanded testimony as to the authority of the Tribal Council to pursue the claim and the authority of the attorneys for the Tribe to represent them in this action.

The government also contended that the Jicarilla Apache claim conflicted with claims of various Pueblo Indians. As a matter of fact, stipulations had been entered into by attorneys for the Jicarilla Apaches and various pueblos along the Rio Grande, stating that the Jicarilla Apaches would not claim any of the Pueblo grant lands.

We explained to the Commission the boundaries of the claim as follows (58 Tr. 8):

> The boundaries set forth in the claim commenced on the southeastern edge at the border of Texas and New Mexico at the 34th Degree and 15th Minute Parallel, and went directly west to a point close to Albuquerque on the edge of the Rio Grande Valley. From there it followed the eastern edge of the valley up to a point just northeast of Albuquerque; and then proceeded in a northeasterly direction to the southern boundary of the Taos Pueblo.
>
> It then followed the southern boundary of the Taos Pueblo southwest, crossing the Rio Grande Valley along and then down to the northern boundary of the Jemez Mountains,

> the Jemez Reservation, and then generally north along the western side of these Pueblo grants along the west of the Chama River watershed to the Continental Divide, and then follows pretty closely the western boundary of the Navajo claim, as we understand it, north to the Colorado border at the 107th Parallel, northeast across the northern end of the San Luis Valley, up to the neighborhood of Pike's Peak, a little north of Pike's Peak, and then along the 39th Parallel to the Colorado, eastern border of Colorado, south along this border on the 102nd degree of Parallel to the Texas border, and then west . . . to the 103rd Parallel and south to the place of beginning.

After this description, the hearing proceeded with the following exchange between Chief Commissioner Edgar E. Witt, Commissioner William M. Holt, and Robert J. Nordhaus (58 Tr. 18):

> **Chief Commissioner Witt:** Involving what acreage?
>
> **Mr. Nordhaus:** A gross acreage of around 46 million.
>
> **Chief Commissioner Witt:** Is your claim of aboriginal title?
>
> **Mr. Nordhaus:** Of aboriginal title? Yes, sir.
>
> **Chief Commissioner Witt:** You do not claim under any recognized title?
>
> **Mr. Nordhaus:** No; not under any recognized title.

Our answer to the question of the chief commissioner as to when the lands were taken from the plaintiff was as follows:

> The government has denied that the lands were taken, and I assume by that they mean that they deny that the petitioner had ever had a claim; but I would say that our contention is that, Mr. Commissioner, number 1, we contend that the lands were taken by the United States, and I do not believe the government disputes that contention, assuming we have a claim.
>
> Secondly, it is our contention that the greater portion, by far the greater portion, of this land, if not all, was taken in the year 1887 when the government placed the Jicarilla

Apache Tribe on its present reservation and, for the first time, kept them there.

Now, we agree that at various times between the American occupation in 1946 when General Kearny marched in—

Chief Commissioner Witt: 1946?

Mr. Nordhaus: 1846; pardon me—and took possession until 1887, that the government temporarily restricted the hunting, gathering activities of this Tribe, and attempted to move them around from one place to another, but the government's attempt to restrict this Tribe were notoriously ineffective all during that period. They tried to move them down to the Mescalero Reservation in southern New Mexico twice, and the first time, somewhere between 800 and 1,200 Indians, they wind up with 37 Indians or so and the chiefs who were down there told the agent they did not know what happened to the other Indians. He could not explain what happened to the other Indians.

In other words, they continued to hunt and gather and continued to engage in some agriculture in their settlements in the very same area that the early Spanish explorers found them as early as the sixteenth century, and I think we will show that there is a continuity of occupation and use there from approximately the earliest records, in the 1598 area of time until 1887, and the only gaps are where the records were not there, and I think Dr. Thomas will explain that.

Chief Commissioner Witt then asked whether the Jicarilla Apache Tribe had ever received any consideration for any of this land. We answered as follows:

That is right, and the Jicarilla Apache—there was never any treaty cession. There was never any consideration whatsoever. The government made treaties but never ratified them. There was never any purchase by the United States of Jicarilla Apache lands, and there are references to that all through the documents.

Commissioner Holt: I take it you contend that the government proceeded to cede the land and convey it to other tribes or other persons?

Mr. Nordhaus: Yes, sir, but generally not until after the Jicarilla Apaches were put on the reservation.

There were undoubtedly homestead entries, railroad grants, grants of portions of this area, prior to 1887, but although we have not secured all the data on this, we feel it is rather small percentage of the total area.

As to the date of taking, if the Commission does not accept the 1887 date, the petitioner will be prepared at a later date to secure the dates of appropriation of land in the area by homestead entry. We have taken samples of certain counties and find that a rather small proportion of the area, particularly in eastern New Mexico, was homesteaded prior to the date that the Jicarilla Apache were put on their reservation.

Commissioner Holt: Was any portion of this land ever ceded by the government to other tribes?

Mr. Nordhaus: There are some rather difficult questions in our minds and apparently in the government's mind as to whether they have.

For instance, in the Ute Treaty of 1863, the government set forth the boundary of the Ute Tribe and it is a little difficult to determine exactly where those boundaries are.

I think possibly the Comanches may have been thought to have ceded some of this land, but our evidence will show that the Comanches at the time of the cession actually did not claim any lands in New Mexico.

The government attorney, William H. Lundin, made an opening statement on behalf of the government. The substance of his statement was that he had not had time to prepare, because the Tribe's claim had been enlarged some twenty times since the original claim, and there was such a vast amount of

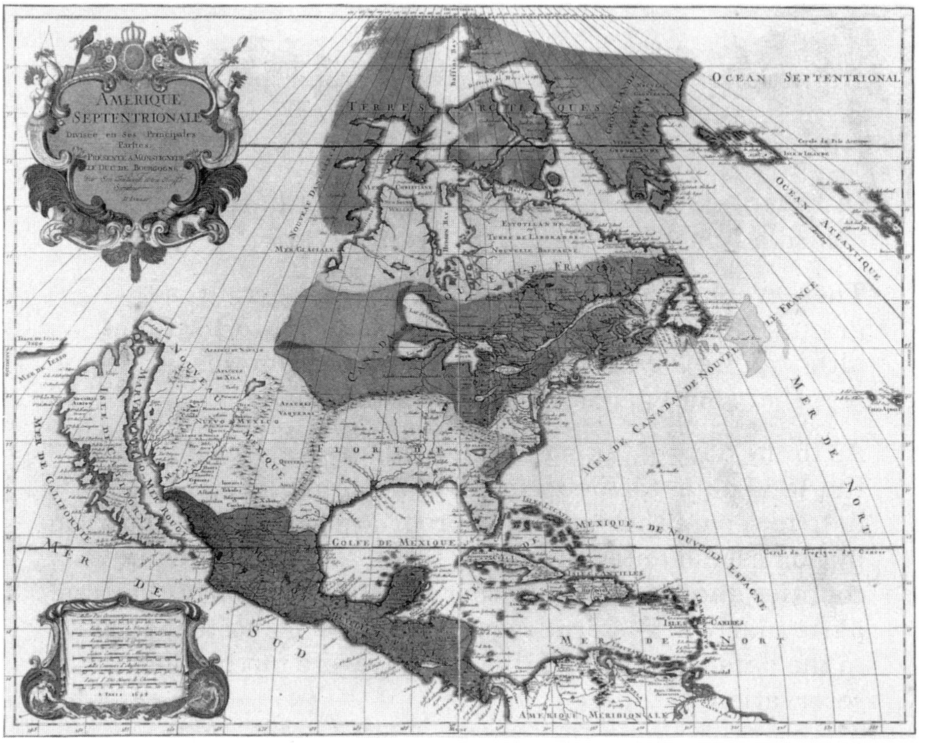

Map 2
H. Jaillot Map of 1694

Map 3
Detail of H. Jaillot Map, Showing Apache Areas

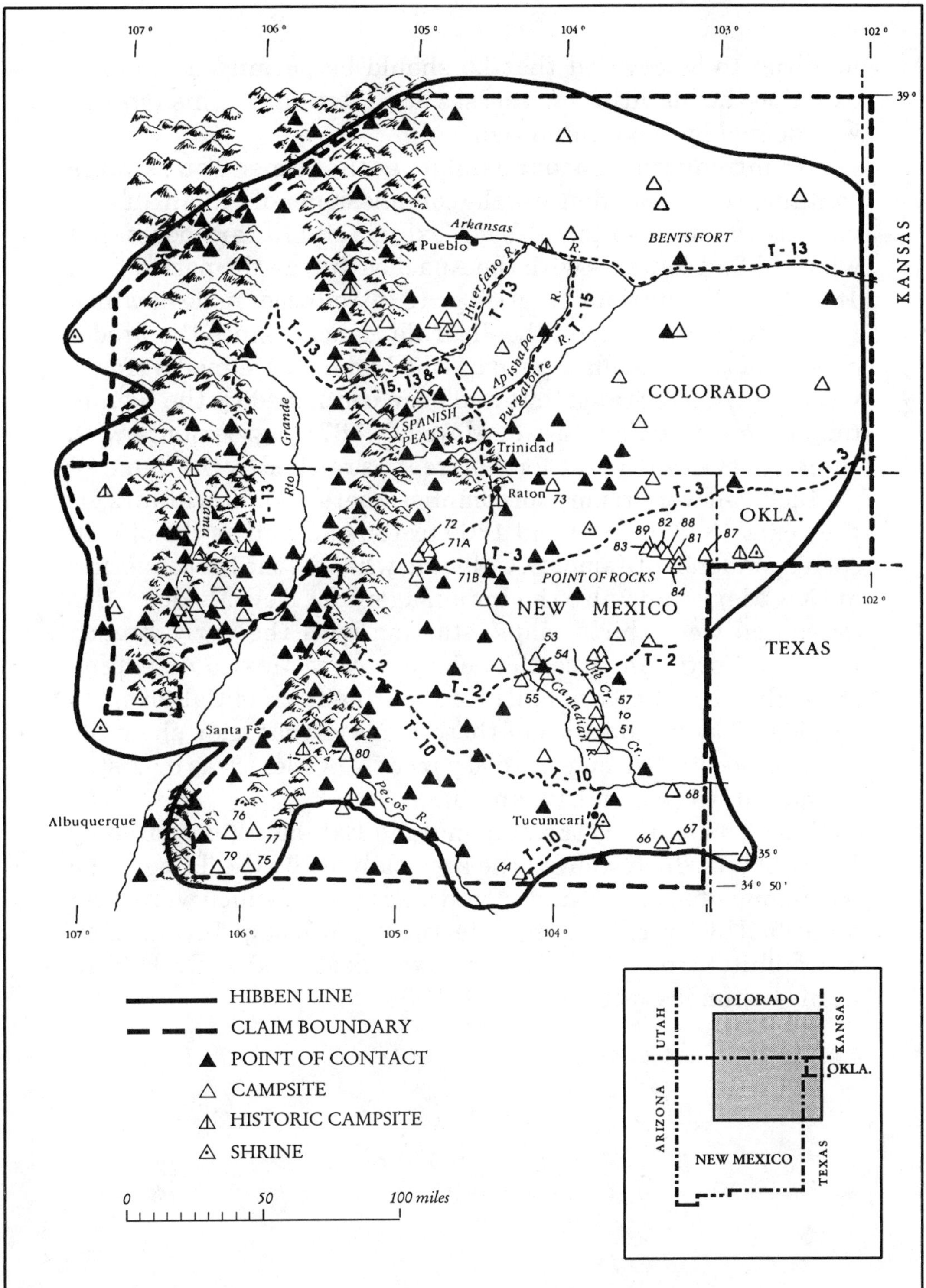

Map 4
Claim Area (Plaintiff's Exhibit M)

material to be covered that he should be permitted to cross-examine the plaintiff's witnesses at a later date. This request was denied by the Commission.

We introduced all of our exhibits at that time. Ten exhibits contained correspondence of the commissioner of Indian affairs, various Indian agents in New Mexico, and military personnel who had had contacts with the Apaches during the period from 1850 to 1887. Various treaties were introduced, none of which had direct bearing upon the Jicarilla Apache, since the predecessors of the Jicarilla Apache Tribe had never signed a treaty with the United States that had been confirmed by the Senate (until the act of Congress of March 3, 1871, agreements with Indian tribes were in the form of treaties ratified by the Senate).

Included were reports of commissioners of Indian affairs for the years 1848 to 1859 and 1860 to 1894 as well as the official correspondence of James S. Calhoun, who was the first governor of New Mexico and also the Indian agent for New Mexico. Also presented were thirty maps, starting with the early French maps of North America that showed New Mexico extending throughout the western half of the continent, from California to Florida. The importance of these maps is that they show the Apaches located through a good part of New Mexico as it existed in those days (see maps 2 and 3).

We also identified the map marked Exhibit M, prepared by Dr. Hibben, which showed the area claimed by the Tribe along with campsites, trails, and sacred places, all of which were later identified by Dr. Hibben in his testimony (see map 4). This map was admitted into evidence after it was described by Dr. Hibben in his testimony of December 4, 1958.

3

• • •

GEOGRAPHY, ETHNOLOGY, AND ARCHAEOLOGY

The geography of the claim area is important in the history of the Jicarilla Apaches (see map 5). The highlands in the western portion of the map comprise a considerable portion of the central section of the claim area in New Mexico and Colorado.

Especially important in the study of the culture of the Jicarilla Apache is the so-called Piedmont Uplift, which is a high plateau, generally level but dropping off in sharp escarpments toward the eastern section of the claim area in New Mexico (see plate 1). The Piedmont Uplift extends along the 103d meridian, from the vicinity of Pritchett in southeastern Colorado, southward to the vicinity of the New Mexico–Oklahoma border, thence in a southwesterly direction, just west of the New Mexico–Texas line to the vicinity of Tucumcari, New Mexico. The plains area of the southwestern United States begins east of the Piedmont.

The terrain of eastern New Mexico restricted the migration of the buffalo herds that in the seventeenth and eighteenth centuries moved north in the spring and south in the fall along the New Mexico–Oklahoma and the New Mexico–Texas borders. Besides being confined to the east by the Piedmont Uplift, the movement of the buffalo was constrained by a number of uncrossable canyons in western Texas. In the southeastern corner of the claim area, the movement of the buffalo was further restricted by the Staked Plains (Llano Estacado)—a series of high mesas that followed a line in a northwesterly to southeasterly direction.

Plate 1
Piedmont Uplift
(courtesy Dr. Frank C. Hibben)

The Jicarilla Apaches camped along the Piedmont Uplift in eastern New Mexico and at the base of the Staked Plains in the southeast portion of the claim during their semiannual buffalo hunts. The Indians were close to the buffalo herds and hunting was relatively easy. In addition the high mesas of the Piedmont and the Staked Plains furnished protection against enemies and provided water. Along the breaks grew juniper and piñon trees, from which the Indians derived nuts and berries as well as wood for fires. The existence of a number of permanent and semipermanent Jicarilla Apache camps shown on map 4 is explained by this topography.

Except for the high mountains of the north-central area of the claim, most of the Jicarilla Apache territory is arid or semiarid. Possible camp and village sites are limited by the availability of water and food. Game in the nineteenth century was scattered and, with the exception of the buffalo in the early decades of the century, extremely scarce; the occurrence of food and game was not dependable. Certain large areas might have a fair crop of nuts and berries in one year, because of abundant rainfall, while other sections of the territory might be completely devoid of food of all kinds.

As a consequence immense stretches of land were required to assure a sufficient food supply each year. Game moved with the availability of moisture, and the Jicarilla Apaches might have to travel several hundred miles to secure good supplies of game. Agriculture was possible only in the river valleys, particularly in the Rio Grande Valley, but the use of major river valleys was generally not available to the Indians at an early date, because of the Spanish settlements and because of the existence of many Indian pueblos.

These geographic factors explain the enormous amount of territory required by the Jicarilla Apaches in their hunting-and-gathering economy. This was an important and valid argument made to convince the Commission that the Tribe needed the large amount of territory included within the claim area.

General Ethnology and Archaeology

Dr. Frank C. Hibben served as expert witness for the Tribe with respect to the anthropology and archaeology substantiating the claim (see plate 2). He made his first study of Jicarilla Apache archaeology in 1933 and had done extensive fieldwork on the archaeology of the Tribe in the claim area since that date. His testimony in this proceeding was based on several facts: his study of the history of the area; his review of authorities on the archaeology and anthropology of the Jicarilla Apaches; information furnished him by very old Indians; and the study of available archaeological information, together with fieldwork done on the archaeology of the Apaches.

The map prepared by Dr. Hibben in connection with his study of the claim area is an enlargement of several U.S.G.S. (United States Geological Survey) survey maps and shows

Map 5
Topographic Map of the Jicarilla Apache Area, Showing the Piedmont Uplift

PIEDMONT UPLIFT
Raton
Cimarron
Springer
Clayton
Wagon Mound
Mora
Las Vegas
Mosquero
Tucumcari
Santa Rosa
Mesa Leon
Vaughn
Fort Sumner
Clovis

Plate 2
Dr. Frank C. Hibben *(courtesy Dr. Frank C. Hibben)*

Jicarilla Apache campsites and villages as tipi symbols accompanied by numbers (map 4). Evidence supporting the identification of these sites as Jicarilla villages or campsites is contained in Dr. Hibben's field notes, prepared in 1957 and 1958. He also referred to his original field notes (prepared in 1933 and 1934), which contained knowledge furnished by his informant, Juan Dedios, and the information gathered through his personal reconnaissance and archaeological fieldwork.

Some of the Jicarilla Apache trails used in hunting and gathering are shown on map 4 as T-3, T-4, T-10, T-13, and T-15;

these and others were described in great detail in Dr. Hibben's testimony. Locations sacred to the Jicarilla Apaches are identified on the map by an asterisk and were also described in the testimony. The heavy black line is the boundary line drawn by Dr. Hibben to mark land exclusively used and occupied by the Jicarilla Apaches up to the time of American occupation and thereafter.

Culture

The Jicarilla Apaches are an Athapascan people, a linguistic group of Indians that probably originated in northwestern Canada. The ancestors of the Jicarilla Apache Tribe evidently moved south along the Rocky Mountains and into the American Southwest between the years 1000 and 1500.

This group included not only the ancestors of the Jicarilla Apache Tribe, but also the Navajos and various bands of Western Apaches. That portion of the Athapascan people who later became known as the Jicarilla Apache Tribe settled throughout the area described as the claim area.

Because of the great distances that separated the various areas of Athapascan settlement, the differences of terrain, and the influences of the cultures of the various groups of Indians whose territories bordered on the area of Athapascan settlement, cultural differences developed among the Athapascans themselves, resulting in a separation of the Athapascans into distinct groups or tribes.

One such identifiable group is the Jicarilla Apaches, who developed a distinctive combination of Plains, Puebloan, and Athapascan traits. In early times, due to close association with the Pueblo Indians, the Jicarilla Apaches developed two outstanding characteristics not generally attributes of other Athapascan tribes. One was a tightly knit tribal organization; the other, the ceremonial division of the tribe into two parts. These two divisions were the "Ollero," or "Mountain," Apaches and the "Llanero," or "Plains," Apaches. In no sense are these

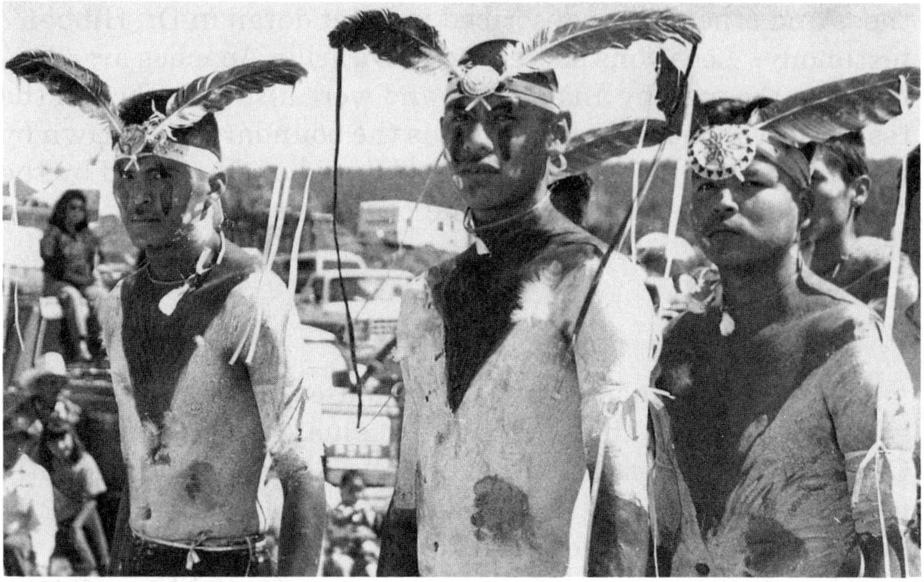

Plate 3
Jicarilla Apache Ceremonial Relay Race Runners

(courtesy *Jicarilla Chieftain*)

Plate 4
A Jicarilla Apache Ceremonial Relay Race, 1992

(courtesy *Jicarilla Chieftain*)

two designations an indication of two separate tribes; they only indicate the part of the Jicarilla Apache territory that each group commonly inhabited. The language, culture, and economy were identical. These two groups were inherently familiar with each other's terrain, commonly hunted together, and engaged in mutual food gathering.

Each of the two groups regularly met for a ceremony and relay race, in which the Olleros ran on one side and the Llaneros on the other. The race was thought to determine whether the gathering or the hunting portion of the economy would fare better in the year to come. It was also an expression of tribal unity and the lack of any real tribal division between the Olleros and Llaneros, as evidenced by the fact that if one side was short of runners, it freely borrowed runners from the other side to complete its relay team.

The relay races continue to this day to be an important feature of the annual feast day of the Jicarilla Apache Tribe, celebrated on September 15 of each year on the reservation (see plates 3–4).

In earlier days the Llaneros and Olleros separated themselves into bands in order to accomplish the mobility that was required of the Jicarilla Apache economy. Originally the bands obtained their names from the places where they lived or from band leaders, but the Spaniards named a great many bands that they encountered in their expeditions in the early eighteenth century.

Dr. Morris E. Opler, a noted anthropologist who produced significant works on Apache culture, identified twelve bands in recent times, six of them operating east of the Rio Grande, six of them west of the river. This band organization was relatively loose and might change from year to year; oftentimes families split off from one band to join another.

The Athapascans were in the American Southwest prior to non-Athapascan impingement on their borders. Non-Athapascans, such as the Comanches and Shoshones, moved across the border into the areas the Jicarilla Apaches had

Plate 5
Jicarilla Apache Pottery
(courtesy Dr. Frank C. Hibben)

exclusively used and occupied. They had different customs and left archaeological evidence of their settlements that was distinguishable from that of the Jicarilla Apaches.

One of these groups, the Utes (a Shoshonean people), bordered Jicarilla Apache land to the northwest. Another group, the Comanches (also of Shoshonean stock), originally impinged on the Jicarillas' northern boundary before migrating in a southeasterly direction. Archaeological sites of the Comanches are known in Texas, but none has yet been identified in New Mexico or Colorado.

The Cheyennes and Arapahoes, members of the large Algonquin-speaking linguistic group of eastern and northern North America, moved southwest toward Jicarilla Apache territory at a relatively late date.

The Kiowa Apaches (unrelated to the Jicarilla Apaches) moved into present-day Oklahoma and Texas from the north, becoming affiliated with the Comanches sometime after 1820.

The culture of the Jicarilla Apaches reflects the influences of the tribes with whom they came into contact. They acquired the art of pottery making at an early date, probably before 1700. Typical Jicarilla micaceous pottery was found in the Dismal River villages, left behind by people identified as Jicarilla Apaches by Dr. Hibben who were influenced by the now-extinct Gallina culture and by the Pueblo Indians. The Jicarilla Apaches developed a variety of distinctive pottery that proved to be very valuable in identifying their villages and campsites (see plate 5).

The Jicarilla Apaches also developed the arts of buffalo hunting and Plains warfare, and the Plains influence is more evident in the Jicarilla Apache way of life than in those of other Athapascan groups.

Pueblo influence was responsible for the introduction of agricultural activity and the moiety system into Jicarilla Apache culture. These traits acquired from other tribes widened the gap between the way of life of the Jicarilla Apaches and that of other Athapascans, such as the Navajos.

Agriculture

Agricultural activities of the Jicarilla Apaches in early times were more extensive than those of other Athapascan groups; Spanish accounts made continual reference to the agricultural pursuits of the Jicarilla Apaches and their predecessor bands. The practice of agriculture was continued to a limited extent during the period of American dominance, generally in the valley of the Cimarron River, where farming was continued into the 1870s, as well as in other locations throughout the claim area. Special Agent William F. N. Arny reported on July 17, 1870, that "these Apaches" roamed throughout the northern portion of the territory of New Mexico. "They plant in patches" and "are a perfect pest to nearly half the population of the territory." Farming was reported as late as 1878 on the Ponil River on the Maxwell Grant.

There is archaeological evidence of agriculture within the claim area around Cimarron, New Mexico. However, the agriculture of the Jicarilla Apaches decreased in economic importance after the early Spanish period. One reason was that the early Spanish and Mexican settlers occupied the valley regions where agriculture was chiefly possible, and the Rio Grande Valley, the major agricultural area in New Mexico, was the domain of various Pueblo tribes. The Jicarilla Apaches were friendly with these tribes, and they did not infringe upon their agricultural lands. The second reason for the decline in agriculture was the increase in the bison herds in the later part of the sixteenth and the early part of the seventeenth centuries. Due to the presence of these large herds, the village agriculture of the plains area generally disappeared, since a ready supply of meat made agriculture unnecessary.

The Sense of Landownership

Because of their agricultural pursuits and Pueblo contacts, the Jicarilla Apaches had a stronger sense of land attachment and landownership than did the Plains tribes such as the Shoshonean peoples. The Jicarilla Apaches had a concept of landownership based upon regular use and occupancy of specific areas for hunting, agriculture, and gathering.

Their concept was not like the modern concept of outright ownership of specifically limited land areas transferable by individuals, nor was it the concept of land use found among nomadic tribes who might roam and wander without regard to where they or their ancestors had been in the past or where their descendants were likely to be in the future.

In the Commission proceedings, Dr. Hibben testified to questions of landownership posed by the court (1958 Tr. 413):

Question: To go on to the relationship in the culture between the Jicarilla and the Pueblo, did the Jicarilla Apache have a developed sense of land ownership?

Answer: I think they did have such a sense of land attachment and land ownership far more than most of the other Athapascans, and certainly more than the Shoshoneans.

Generally, a land organization which is almost entirely nomadic and mobile does not make a strong attachment to the land. The Utes who were very mobile and practiced a hunting and gathering economy had very little, if any, attachment to the land because if the land did not produce food at that time they did not call it their own.

The Jicarilla, probably from Pueblan sources, had a strong sense of attachment and family bands became identified in particular areas. This was especially true when they practiced agriculture.

In my opinion, I would say that the Indian tribes in the southwestern area who had a great sense of land ownership were probably, for the most part, the Pueblo who were sedentary and who farmed the land year after year, and second to the Pueblo would be the Jicarilla Apache because of the reasons I have just stated.

Certain of the other Athapascan groups who were much more mobile and whose tribal organization was more loosely knit had a much weaker attachment to any particular land or topography or terrain.

Question: Has your study of the Jicarilla Apache indicated that they conducted their activities over the same general area for a long period of time?

Answer: That is true. The various bands which we can identify stayed in certain areas, meeting together for annual or semiannual ceremonies and then returning to their particular regions.

In the early days, when agriculture was a prevalent base of their economy, the attachment was especially strong in certain fields which were farmed by the same Jicarilla families year after year, and they even constructed irrigation systems which were considerably elaborate.

In the seventeenth, eighteenth, and nineteenth centuries

the Jicarilla Apaches roamed over and utilized an extremely large area of land. But their activities were carried out on a definite and regular basis. For example, they had permanent villages in the mountainous areas of northern New Mexico, where the land was utilized extensively for houses and for the growing of crops. Members of the tribe lived in adobe or stone houses in these villages and engaged in agricultural pursuits. Other portions of the claim area, mainly the more distant mountain regions, were used periodically and regularly for gathering berries, nuts, and other wild foods, and the Jicarilla regarded these areas as their own lands, taking food from them whenever the supply was sufficient.

Regular buffalo hunts were conducted on the eastern plains in the spring and fall of each year, and although the Jicarilla Apaches were not constantly on the land, they regarded it as belonging to them for the purpose most useful to them, namely that of supplying them with meat, hides, and other benefits obtained from the buffalo.

In addition to fulfilling the necessities of Indian life, the land in the claim area held a religious significance for the Jicarilla Apaches, because their ancestors were buried there and because their folklore revolved about specific places on the land, such as the Jemez Mountains, from which the Jicarillas believed all life on earth had originated.

The tribe's creation legend located their territory in southeastern Colorado and northern New Mexico, and the Arkansas, Rio Grande, and Canadian rivers figured in their genesis myth (Hodge, *Handbook* 1:631–52).

The Jicarilla Apaches also regarded numerous places within the claim area as having religious significance, such as Pike's Peak, the Cave of the Winds (near Colorado Springs), Tucumcari Butte, and Sierra Blanca (north of La Veta Pass on the Colorado–New Mexico border). They defended their homeland with fanaticism and devotion against other Indian tribes, as well as against American military forces.

Even after these Apaches were defeated by the United States Army forces in the 1850s, their actions and words indicated a continuing desire to remain in their ancestral territory.

Warfare

The Jicarilla Apaches developed a distinctive method of warfare. In his testimony before the Commission, Dr. Hibben stated (1958 Tr. 437):

> **Question:** Would you summarize their method of warfare?
>
> **Answer:** The warfare of the Jicarilla was a plains acquisition. They derived this from their contact with the plains tribes and, of course, the warfare of the plains is an outstanding characteristic of the plains area. This warfare was made very much accentuated by the acquisition of the horse. When they were all on foot in the early days, they could not travel the distances to be in contact with one another.
>
> Plains warfare is based chiefly on the counting of coup which is a French expression meaning a blow. The plains tribes practiced the counting of coup which meant the touching of an enemy with a weapon. Now, the killing of an enemy was not so meritorious as touching the enemy. This was the way they acquired social prestige.
>
> After the engagement, the group returned to their camp and counted coup which was the retelling of these experiences, all of which had to be accentuated. This counting of coup was developed by the Jicarilla Apache to a very limited extent. They did count coup. They were people who took scalps as part of this same characteristic.
>
> Now, the taking of scalps is a relatively modern development. In the early days, they took the whole head or the hands or the feet. The taking of the scalp was a neat way of bringing back the booty.
>
> The Jicarilla Apache were caught between the two ceremonial groups, on the one hand the Athapascan with a fear of death, and the Apache and the Navajo have the same

> characteristic and are very much afraid of a dead person or a place where a person has died.
>
> The plains counting of coup was in direct conflict with this. Usually when the Jicarilla Apache had made a successful raid they would get one person to collect the scalps and to keep them until they all had been purified, which is a sort of a combination arrangement between a plains hunting ceremony and typical Athapascan fear of death. The Jicarilla, I think, generally were not very much oriented toward warfare. Chiefly, their warfare was defensive. They put up a fight which lasted over a great many decades, keeping the Comanches out of their terrain and, to a lesser extent, the Americans.

The location of village sites in eastern New Mexico, on the edge of the Piedmont Uplift, made it more possible for the Jicarilla Apaches to defend themselves from raids of enemy tribes from the east. Smoke signals were used as a means for communication in both defensive and offensive warfare. When caught between opposing ceremonial traits, such as the Athapascan fear of death and the Plains characteristic of collecting scalps, the Jicarilla Apaches would effect a compromise.

The weapons of the Apaches were lances and bows and arrows, varying in size according to the group who used them. Among the Plains Indians there were some firearms, but these were seldom used, because ammunition was scarce and there was no way to repair them when broken. The Indians often used the metal from the weapons to make lances, arrowheads, and other implements (see plates 6–7).

Social Structure

The Jicarilla Apaches had a social structure based on a loosely knit organization which was "matrilinear" (reckoning descent through the maternal line) and also matrilocal (customarily the young married people lived with the bride's mother). Addressing this, Dr. Hibben testified (1958 Tr. 419):

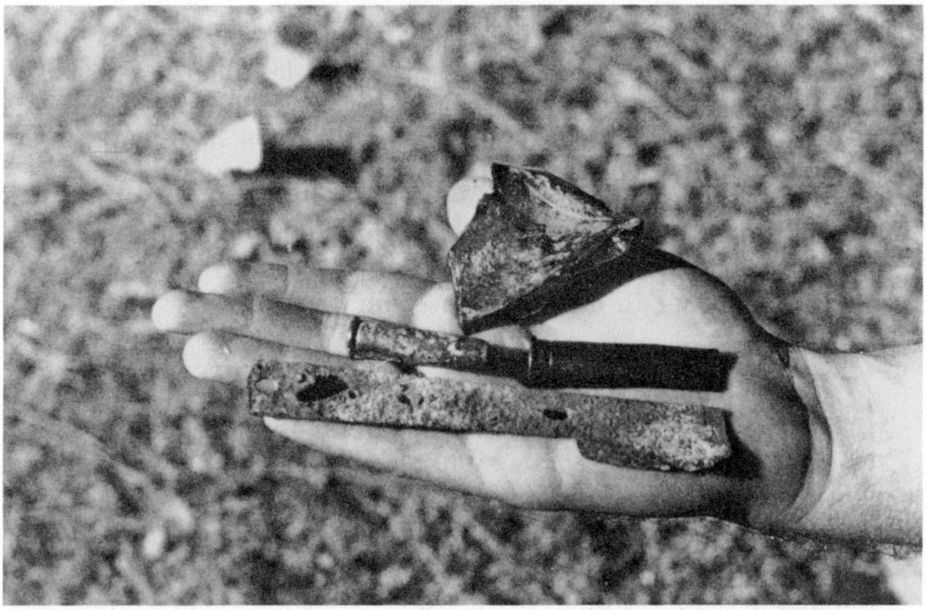

Plate 6 *(courtesy Dr. Frank C. Hibben)*
Cartridge Cases, Knife, and Scraper

Plate 7 *(courtesy Dr. Frank C. Hibben)*
Iron Arrowhead in Buffalo Bone

> **Question:** Will you explain matrilinear?
>
> **Answer:** That is descent through the female line. The arrangement was to live with your mother-in-law, although they practiced mother-in-law avoidance, which seems to be logical and in keeping with the Navajo.
>
> Their camps are usually close enough to keep cohesion, and yet the husbands have their lodges separated far enough so that this mother-in-law avoidance can be practiced.
>
> The matrilocal nature of their camps is also a marked Athapascan characteristic. When a young man gets married, he goes to live with his wife's family and the band would consist of the female siblings which is simply the female descendants and, of couse, the unmarried people, which is a very strong characteristic of the Jicarilla, have a reliance upon the grandparents. The grandparents are the important people which, I think, also is logical. The young children, for example, are practically brought up by the grandparents, especially the matrilinear grandparent, and there is always this emphasis on the matrilinear side of the descent.

A typical Jicarilla Apache group consisted of a family in a direct matrilineal line, with unmarried sons and daughters in attendance and sons-in-law and married daughters living in separate families, but remaining close enough to the family camp to maintain cohesion. Children were instructed and actually raised by their grandparents, leaving their parents free to hunt and gather. Grandparents in turn depended on the young boys to provide small game for them.

The concept of a supreme being is found in Jicarilla Apache religion; this being was recognized as both a punisher and rewarder. Although influenced to some extent by Catholicism, they were never converted to that religion.

Dancing was a form of Apache diversion with ceremonial significance. Their own voices and the beating of sticks on a tight skin attached to a gourd provided the only music. Jicarilla

Apache crafts included basket weaving and pottery making, and tribal members collected feathers for ornamental purposes and for use in arrow making.

Antonio Cordero's description of the Apaches is a valuable source of information as to the culture of the Apaches during Spanish times. He describes the dress of the men and women, their arms, the dwelling places, and the gathering of their bands. The dress of the Jicarilla Apache women was elaborate. They wore dresses of skins with short skirts tied at the waist and a skirt or coat drawn over the head, hanging to the waist, with the shoulders and sides open. Their hair was tied with a bag of deer, buffalo, or other animal hide. They wore ornaments on their necks and arms of deer and antelope hooves, shells, fish bones, and the roots of sweet-smelling herbs.

The men had no obligation to the family economy other than that of hunting and fighting and making weapons, saddles, and other trappings necessary for raids. The women took care of their animals, made utensils, cured and tanned hides, carried water and firewood, and gathered seeds and fruits, which they dried to make bread and cakes. They sowed corn and beans where agriculture was practiced. They also accompanied their husbands on expeditions, driving stolen animals, aiding in ceremonials, and serving in whatever other capacity was required of them.

Cordero described the location of the dwelling places of the Apaches, their movements, and the area of land they required. Cordero's firsthand report is important, not only for its historical value, but also in establishing the tremendous territory required by the early bands of Apaches in order to sustain themselves (Matson and Schroeder, eds., "Cordero's Description of the Apache"):

> In general, they chose for dwelling places the most rugged and mountainous ranges. In these places they found water and wood in abundance, and the wild terrain produced natural fortifications where they could defend themselves from their enemies. Their hovels or huts were circular,

made of branches of trees covered with skins of horses, cows or bison—many used tents of this type.

In the cạnyons of the mountain ranges the men sought large and small game—proceeding as far as the contiguous plains. When they obtained what was necessary, they brought it back to their camp where it was the work of the women, not only to prepare the foods, but also to tan the skins which were used for a multitude of purposes—particularly for clothing.

They would change their *rancherías* when their location, in which they have been living, could no longer provide enough foods necessary for their needs. They would then move from one mountain range to the other; or, perhaps, from one rock or cliff to another within the same mountain range. Moves were also influenced by the necessity to seek places where they could spend the different seasons of the year with more comfort.

The number of their population did not correspond in any way, whatsoever, to the territory they occupied. This is the reason for the spacious deserts which are found in this enormous country, and for the fact that every family head in his camp considered himself a sovereign in his district.

Plains Culture and Buffalo Hunting

Dr. Hibben, in describing the culture of the Jicarilla Apaches, mentioned that in the course of centuries, although they were first an agricultural tribe, they later developed Plains characteristics, which meant that as soon as the buffalo arrived in great numbers in the eighteenth century, the Jicarilla Apaches started hunting them. He testified as follows (1958 Tr. 423):

> A significant effect of the coming of the bison herds—the buffalo, of course, was not a true buffalo—is an interesting story which goes back to the Ice Age when there were many buffalo in this area of the country. The descendants of these buffalo became the modern bison, of which we are familiar, and though they were present in the plains area

in early times, and Coronado mentioned them in 1541 and called them cows, they were not present in great numbers. They were scattered, otherwise the village cultures of the plains would not have existed.

You are probably well aware that in the plains area, especially in the Missouri Valley and on the Republican and various rivers in Kansas, Nebraska and Iowa, there were people—during the 12th, 13th and 14th century [living in] village cultures. They created permanent villages, and they made pottery and had many sedentary characteristics. The agriculture which the villages practiced would have been almost impossible with large bison herds. They did not have barbed wire fences and the bison would have made short work of their cornfields.

The bison increased very greatly for some unknown reason, probably in the last half of the 16th century and the beginning of the 17th century, probably some time after Coronado made his trip into the western plains. The increase of the bison herds brought a change in village cultures, not all of them, but most of them, and made village agriculture unnecessary. It represented a tremendous supply of meat in the form of these bison herds which is an economic asset in itself.

The Jicarilla Apache in the region of El Quartalejo which has been located in Scott County, Kansas, were carrying on village cultures at this time. Lacking interference from present herds and from movements of other tribes, it might have been developed into a purely agricultural tribe. As it was, the increase of these bison herds set in motion many of the movements which we have mentioned, namely that the tribes on the periphery of the plains began to move into the plains in search of two things. The major item was buffalo and the meat presented by this enormous supply of food on the hoof, and the other was the excitement of the chase. It was a lot more fun to hunt buffalo than to grow corn.

Thus the Plains cultures developed and became an outstanding aspect of the whole region. The Jicarillas were on the

Plate 8
Juan Dedios

(courtesy National Archives, Washington, D.C.)

periphery of the region and thus developed some of these characteristics, but not all of them.

The notes Dr. Hibben took in 1933 describing his conversations with Juan Dedios, the old Indian, are interesting in this connection (Pet. Exh. S) (see plate 8):

> Bull buffalo—winter robes; cow buffalo—tents; eat hump first—then stomach; use stomach for sack; skin legs of bull buffalo for moccasins.
>
> Big camps and places where lots of firewood and water. Also, good place to see enemy and fight enemy. Big camps on mesas or rocks.
>
> Stay away from trails from forts. Many soldiers there. Always trouble.
>
> Scrape skins with stone scraper—women.
>
> Put bones in [one] place so buffalo not get angry and not get killed again.
>
> Elk, skin from back; make shirts of skin; dry meat for winter food. Antelope skinned from belly; eat antelope fresh—no good for drying.
>
> Trade dry meat in Taos to wagons at Rayado.

This is typical of the Juan Dedios notes, which provided vivid pictures of the hunting habits and travels of the Jicarilla Apaches. Dr. Hibben testified as follows in regard to the movements of the Plains tribes (1958 Tr. 425):

> The Comanches moved east and out on the plains, developing plains character—and by plains characteristics, I mean buffalo hunting with everything that goes with it.
>
> The advent of the horse, of course, added to the mobility of the tribes. They could carry more meat and could hunt better, and could move greater distances, and with changed type of warfare.
>
> The Jicarilla Apaches were on the periphery of this situation. In the area that we are interested in there was a major migration of the buffalo.

> The so-called western herd of buffalo, which at times numbered several million animals, migrated north and south in the spring and fall about the line between New Mexico and Texas.
>
> Accounts of informants say that it was east of Logan, New Mexico at a place called Buffalo Crossing. [That is, about the southeast corner of the claim area.]
>
> The buffalo migrated north in the spring with the greening of the grass through what is now the panhandle of Oklahoma and up into southeastern Colorado. The terrain constricted the herds in what was eastern New Mexico and western Texas.

Dr. Hibben testified that the permanent villages of the Jicarilla Apaches were established in places which were defensible and had water and wood. In these permanent villages, they left the grandparents with the children during the buffalo hunts and during other times when the parents were absent. The young children, especially the young boys, supported the older people in gathering and hunting wild game. Able-bodied men with a number of horses would go out on a hunt, taking with them their wives and the young girls to do the work.

Buffalo hunts took place at some distance from the permanent villages. The base camps for buffalo hunts were generally located along the edge of the Piedmont, in eastern New Mexico. Various sites located by Dr. Hibben from information furnished by Juan Dedios are shown on map 4.

During the seasonal hunt, a band of Jicarilla Apaches might travel several hundred miles from the extreme western portions of the claim area to the eastern buffalo-hunting area; after the hunt they would bring dried meat back to the mountains of the western area of the claim. This dried meat was their major source of food for the following season.

The various bands of Jicarilla Apaches had base camps located throughout the claim area that were shown to be good spots for their semiannual buffalo hunts that were conducted during the spring and fall seasons. Of these two seasons, the fall hunt was the most important, because the buffalo were usually fat at that time.

In the spring, the buffalo were thin and the cows were heavy with calves; they generally made very poor meat. But the buffalo was the most important item in the economy of the Jicarilla Apaches and the other Plains tribes and was the source of many items of clothing and shelter in addition to being a staple article of diet. The information given by Juan Dedios to Dr. Hibben in 1933 on buffalo hunting is very informative (Pet. Exh. S):

> Apache plains people go east and make camp—live like other plains people and move tipis easy, camp near water. Take young women for slavery and work. Old women and men in big camp would spend winter.
>
> Big camps and places where lots of firewood and water. Also, good place to see enemy and fight enemy. Big camps on mesas or rocks.
>
> Hunt buffalo in herds. Juan leader of hunt, had Spanish gun. Sometimes could shoot several buffalo from behind rocks—rest not scared. Drive herd past hunters waiting on horses. Gallop out with bows and arrows. Arrows with iron heads made from wagon tires. Not use stone points anymore—used to! . . .
>
> Built houses on top of mesas for winter—tipis for summer. Many enemies go up and down Ute Creek. Jicarillas and some Utes have big fights with Comanches here—drove Comanches back to east.
>
> From Tres Mesas de la Trinidad (Dead Man's Mesas), parties go east to hunt buffalo. Take young women to do skinning and work—leave old women, men and children on Tres Mesas.
>
> Buffalo camps need good horses. Best buffalo hunting to northeast—depends on season. Buffalo moves south in big herds and fall—this time—November.
>
> Shoot buffalo with arrows from horseback. Iron arrows are best—made from wagon tires.

> Held big race at Tres Mesas between two teams—red and white—Mountain Apaches and Plains Apaches. Race to see if there would be good buffalo hunting. Racers go from two corrals along track. Juan showed me corral at base of mesa.
>
> Followed down trail to Tucumcari Butte to put hands on sacred rock there. Then hunted buffalo to east—and winter buffalo south of deep canyon beyond Red River. Brought back much dried meat to camp on Largo. Corn mixed with buffalo meat is cooked.
>
> Necessary to ask for forgiveness of buffalo after killing them. Buffalo once people and people were hunted. Then people became powerful and hunted animals, but necessary that animal not be angry after kill.
>
> Tucumcari Butte—landmark of Apaches—were afraid to go out on eastern buffalo hunt because got lost and hard to find water after crossing Canadian. Tucumcari Butte landmark—seldom went hunting farther than could see top of this landmark.
>
> Stone on side of Tucumcari Butte very sacred. Before buffalo hunt, every hunter laid hands on this stone to add good luck in hunt. While hunter was hunting to northeast, his wife touched the rock and prayed to it.
>
> One time, east of Tucumcari Butte, Juan and Jicarillas found a whole herd of buffalo mired in river bottom. Killed them all—could not butcher them all—bad hunting next year because of this. When Jicarillas go to war against enemies, have special words which are used.

The Jicarilla Apaches, although they had a number of Plains characteristics such as hunting buffalo, the use of the tipi, the use of the travois, and the use of the parfleche (leather envelope for carrying dried buffalo meat), were never completely a Plains tribe, and they were never completely mobile. They set out on a buffalo hunt from fixed villages, and their mobility was within certain limits.

Unlike the more typical Plains tribes, the Jicarilla Apaches carried their pottery with them, since the hunting trips took them only a limited distance from their fixed villages.

Dwellings

In pursuing the land claim, archaeological and historical evidence of exclusive use and occupancy of the claim area was supported by the identification of specific Jicarilla Apache campsites and village sites. The tribe relied on this identification, based both on archaeological evidence as presented by its expert witness, Dr. Hibben, and the testimony of aged Indians and other informants.

The way of life and customs of the Jicarilla Apaches were sufficiently distinct from those of other tribes to permit old campsites to be definitely established as Jicarilla sites on the basis of artifacts found there. Dr. Hibben testified that the combination of certain characteristic features made it possible to positively identify Jicarilla Apache village sites. These characteristic features included house types, pottery, grinding equipment, and burial procedures.

The corroboration supplied by the archaeological evidence (the campsites found by Dr. Hibben and the characteristic features of Jicarilla Apache archaeology), the information supplied by Juan Dedios, and the historical evidence of Spanish and American contacts with Jicarillas all established without a doubt the extent of Jicarilla activities in the claim area.

Four Jicarilla Apache house types were used during recorded history. The vestiges of many of these dwellings were found by Dr. Hibben during his reconnaissance of the claim area.

The first type was the flat-roofed adobe structure mentioned in early Spanish accounts as a ranchería. This type of house was abandoned in the latter part of the eighteenth century.

The Jicarilla Apaches also used a type of hogan as a ceremonial house, distinguishable from the Navajo hogan on the basis of size, superstructure, and positioning of interior features. Several of these hogan structures, identified by stone rings and piles, were found by Dr. Hibben in his archaeological study of the claim area.

A third type of habitation was the brush lodge, which was circular, with an opening toward the east, dome shaped, covered with skins and bark and sometimes with earth, and usually surrounded by a ring of earth and a ring of stone. This type of housing was used within the memory of living Indian informants. The remains of these structures could be identified by a semicircle of stones with an opening to the east or southeast (see plates 9–10).

The most common type of dwelling prior to the establishment of the reservation was the tipi, made of buffalo skins and erected on poles. Jicarilla Apache tipi sites are identified by a ring of stones placed around the base of the buffalo skin forming the covering of the tipi (see plates 11–13).

The doorway of Jicarilla tipis was always located to the east or southeast, an Athapascan trait not typical of any of the Plains Indians on the border of the Jicarilla Apache claim area.

Pottery

Pottery is a major archaeological identification tool, since its manufacture is characteristic, so that particular pottery can generally be traced to a particular tribe of Indians. Jicarilla pottery is of two types.

First is a thin pottery, dark in color, tempered with flecks of mica that make it sparkle. The vases or vessels of this type are pointed at the bottom. This pottery is generally associated with the Dismal River culture of the western plains area.

The other type of pottery is somewhat thicker, lighter in color, and also tempered with mica and generally of the same shape. This type of pottery also has a relatively narrow neck; it is closely associated with the pottery of Taos and Picuris pueblos (plate 5).

Plate 9
Frame of Traditional Brush Shelter
(courtesy Dr. Frank C. Hibben)

Plate 10
Remnants of Brush Shelter
(courtesy Dr. Frank C. Hibben)

Plate 11
Tipi Rings, Probably from Sweatlodge
(courtesy Dr. Frank C. Hibben)

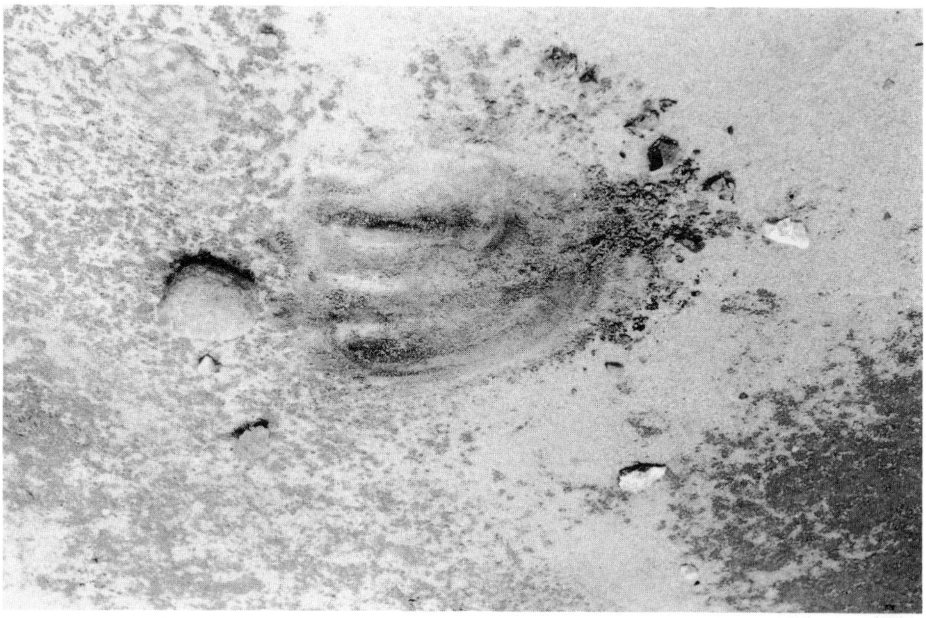

Plate 12
Tipi Rings and Fire Pit
(courtesy Dr. Frank C. Hibben)

Plate 13 *(courtesy Dr. Frank C. Hibben)*
Tipi Rings, Dead Man's Mesa

The pottery of the Jicarilla Apaches is readily distinguishable from Navajo pottery and is a primary criterion for distinguishing Jicarilla sites from non-Athapascan sites, because non-Athapascans (excepting the Pueblo Indians) made little or no pottery.

The Cheyenne Indians lost the art of making pottery in their early antiquity, the Comanches were not known to make pottery at all, and the Utes made very little. Pottery is thus a major artifact identifying Jicarilla Apache sites.

Miscellaneous Campsite Evidence

Grinding equipment, particularly the one-handed mano, is typical of a gathering economy such as that of the Jicarilla Apaches. While the equipment itself is difficult to distinguish from that of other tribes that utilize grinding tools, its presence at camp sites bordering the area of the Plains tribes is indicative of Jicarilla Apache occupancy.

Another identifying characteristic of Jicarilla Apache campsites was the lack of human and animal bones in the vicinity. Jicarilla Apaches retained the Athapascan trait of fear of death, and they never buried their members nearby. Similarly animal bones were always placed at a distance from the village on one single pile, for ceremonial reasons. Cheyenne and Comanche sites, on the other hand, habitually show a litter of buffalo bones and other debris.

While traveling with Dr. Hibben in 1933 over a major portion of the Jicarilla Apache claim area, Juan Dedios pointed out to him numerous Jicarilla Apache trails, sacred places, and a large number of village sites occupied by the Jicarilla Apaches on their hunts.

In preparation for his testimony in this case, Dr. Hibben revisited these sites, making fieldnotes and taking photographs. He also verified the information by evaluating the sites and by studying the artifacts he found. Where no informants were involved, sites were identified by a combination of archaeological data including house types, pottery, grinding equipment, scrapers, and other artifacts (plates 5–7 and 9–14).

Dr. Hibben testified that he was certain as to the correct identification of all the Jicarilla Apache sites located by tipi symbols in exhibit M (map 4). The sites shown on this map were occupied by the Jicarilla Apaches over long periods of time, from the Spanish occupation or earlier, through the 1870s. One site was at least two hundred years old and showed evidence of comparatively recent occupancy.

The identification by Dr. Hibben of a large number of such archaeological sites provided evidence that the Jicarilla Apaches regularly hunted on the eastern plains and gathered and hunted in the entire claim area long before the date of the United States occupancy of New Mexico from 1846 through the 1870s. Certain sites located by Dr. Hibben could be dated with reasonable accuracy from the historical material found there—Spanish trade items, American-period cartridge cases, bottle glass, beads, and other trade goods.

Plate 14
Stone Scrapers
(courtesy Dr. Frank C. Hibben)

Sacred Places and Landmarks

Places and landmarks sacred to the Jicarilla Apaches were identified by Dr. Hibben and strongly supported the Tribe's claim. Those described by Juan Dedios were La Veta Butte, Sierra Blanca (north of La Veta Pass; see plate 15), Huerfano Butte (south of Pueblo, Colorado; see plate 16), Cave of the Winds (at Colorado Springs), and Tucumcari Butte (in northeastern New Mexico).

Some of these sacred places were identified by testimony of elders of the tribe who had learned of them from their fathers and grandfathers. Others were identified by Juan Dedios in statements to Dr. Hibben, such as the following (Pet. Exh. S):

> **Spanish Peaks** were called "mountains which hold up sky." Juan said that there were many sheep there. They had a separate special camp for men who were going to hunt mountain sheep. They used separate words for mountain sheep. They never called them by name. This would scare

Plate 15
Sierra Blanca in Winter
(courtesy Emily Tiller)

Plate 16
Huerfano Butte
(courtesy Dr. Frank C. Hibben)

them off. After the hunt, they would return the bones to the mountain.

Huerfano Butte [plate 16]. They camped on the lower Huerfano River to hunt elk. "They would always stop there and touch stone for good luck in hunting." The Apaches went from Huerfano Butte down to the Apiscapa River, to the Napesta [Arkansas River]. Juan said, "Best place for elk here; many deer on river bottom—east of river and north, buffalo. Also many enemies. Juan and Luna hunted elk at Apiscapa the year after great war [Civil War], killed over 100 elk."

Rabbit Ear Mountain. Juan said, "Good buffalo hunting at Buffalo Springs south of Rabbit Ear—camped here—Rabbit Ear sacred place—leave buffalo bones here and offering to spirit."

Tucumcari Butte. Juan said, "Follow down trail to Tucumcari Butte to put hands on the sacred rock there. Then hunted buffalo to east—and winter buffalo south of deep canyon beyond Red River [Canadian River]."

Trails

Dr. Hibben identified some of the trails that were used by the Jicarilla Apaches in going from one hunting ground to another. These were pointed out to him by Juan Dedios; he covered many of these trails with Juan in 1933 (map 4):

T-3: From Cimarron to Point of Rocks to the Big Cimarron, used by the Jicarillas in traveling from the settlements in the vicinity of Taos to the buffalo-hunting grounds to the east.

T-4: Trail through Raton Pass east of Raton, New Mexico to the Spanish Peaks in Colorado, used by the Apaches en route to the sheep-hunting grounds in the northern mountains.

T-10: Along the Canadian River to Tucumcari Mountain, then south to Logan, where the major buffalo herds passed on their north-south migrations.

T-13: One of the major trails to the north led to the north-central portion of the claim area, to the San Luis Valley, and extended in a northerly and northeasterly direction across Mosca Pass, thence down the Huerfano River and into the plains, along the Arkansas River.

T-15: Led from the vicinity of the Spanish Peaks in a northeasterly direction, down the Apiscapa River and thence to the Arkansas River.

Permanent and Semipermanent Village Sites

In the southern and eastern areas of the claim, many permanent and semipermanent village sites were located by Dr. Hibben, generally on high ground, where the Indians could view a large expanse of terrain and where there was wood and water. Such sites were on Crow Butte (site no. 77; see plate 17) and Lobo Hill (site no. 75), both commanding a view of the entire expanse of the Estancia Valley as far west as the Sandia Mountains. From the top of Lobo Hill, one could see as far as the southern boundary of the claim.

Many of these sites had evidence of ancient and long-continued Jicarilla occupancy extending well into the American period. Among the important village sites in the southeastern part of the claim were the southern sites of Ima, Tucumcari Butte, and San Jon.

The Ima site is at the edge of the Piedmont and consists of one thousand or more tipi rings; it shows considerable evidence of long prehistoric and historic occupation. Evidence was found that the band of the Jicarilla chief Chino camped there in the winter of 1878–79. Archaeological evidence also indicates that this site was used for many years before and after this date. It is typical of sites selected by the Apaches because it was close to the buffalo herds, gave protection against enemies, and provided abundant wood and water.

Plate 17 *(courtesy Dr. Frank C. Hibben)*
Crow Butte

Hunting Encampments

Dr. Hibben identified more than twenty permanent or semipermanent Jicarilla Apache hunting encampments, located in eastern New Mexico along the edge of the Piedmont Uplift on high mesas overlooking the buffalo plains. The sites around Gallegos were typical of hunting camps on the edge of the Piedmont. A similar cluster of sites was discovered north of Clayton, New Mexico, and other large semipermanent sites were found near Gallegos. These encampments afforded an unlimited view of the buffalo plains, with good protection from enemies. Mesas of the Trinity (Dead Man's Mesa) were defensible places on high ground with a number of permanent dwellings that showed evidence of occupancy over a long period of time (plate 13).

Mountain Camps

In the mountainous portion of the central area of the claim were found a number of other sites. Typical of those sites on the eastern slope of the mountains were those on Rattlesnake Butte. These defensive sites were on high ground, from which the Indians could see for long distances; they commanded an undulating plain where there was very good hunting for elk and antelope, along with some buffalo hunting. The Jicarilla Apaches had permanent villages on these sites.

There were also various sites on the western slope of the mountains surrounding the San Juan Valley. The Culebra Creek site was used as a common camping place by the Tribe when they moved north to the San Luis Valley to hunt in the mountains for antelope and mountain sheep. It was apparently the camping place of the Acho Apaches mentioned by Don Diego de Vargas in 1696, and it was also regularly used during the historic times.

Other sites used by the Apaches as they traveled north to hunt mountain sheep and other game in the Sangre de Cristos in Colorado were discovered on Indian Creek—one north of Fort Garland, one at Red Wing, and one north of the Huerfano River.

The archaeological evidence of occupancy at these sites includes pottery (both Jicarilla and Spanish), manos, scrapers, broad-bladed arrowheads (some of iron), brass dangles, tipi rings, and camp debris. These sites were pointed out by Juan Dedios as camping places of the Jicarilla Apaches when they traveled from New Mexico into Colorado to hunt mountain sheep and when they moved into the Huerfano Valley.

The presence of Spanish-type pottery, as well as modern tools, indicates the use of these sites from the Spanish period through American times. Accounts of the hunting-and-gathering activities of the Jicarilla Apaches furnished by Juan Dedios and encounters of the Spanish explorers and early American expeditions provide evidence of the extent of the territory utilized by the Apaches in their various activities. According to Juan Dedios (Pet. Exh. S):

Go out buffalo hunting to eat, hunting mountain sheep to north by Blanco Mountain beyond San Luis.

Pecos Mountains and north to Windy mountains better for mountain food. In Pecos get choke cherries, acorns, tree bark, pinon nuts, herbs for medicines. Go in from Mora side or north. Some Apaches stay there all the time hunting deer, elk, traded medicine plants for buffalo meat.

Apaches had to grow corn. Many had corn fields along Cimarron near Cimarron town.

Apaches and Utes not like to grow corn. Rather hunt buffalo, antelope, mountain sheep.

Mountain sheep huntings in Windy Mountains [Wet Mountains and Spanish Peaks].

Icy mountains north of San Luis good place for sheep—camp at Red Wing. Go on trail past Spanish peaks, cross Bent's Fort. Trail at night—go up river past Huerfano Butte. Big camp here for Cimarrones [mountain sheep], also piñon nuts and deer, get bark of trees in Windy mountains. Trail from Cimarron to point of rocks and to buffalo grounds.

Camped on Rio Puerco—go from here to Abiquiu. Trail down river to cross to Taos to raid. Trail to buffalo grounds along Red River [Canadian] to town of Cimarron. Rations at Abiquiu and Cimarron. Trails from Cimarron to point of rocks and to buffalo grounds (do not cross Raton pass of Bent's Fort trail—many soldiers—no game!).

Trail from Mora to Red River [Canadian]—crossing at ford—camp here. Place to take horses across. Trail to Tres Mesas de la Trinidad—Gallegos store to winter camping place.

Hunting in Estancia Valley antelope—many there, fight at stone house between Homestead and Circle Dot Ranches.

Juan said the Apaches camped at the north end of the Estancia Valley and made raids from there along the Rio

Grande. He had camped near Stanley and stolen horses at Bernalillo (Pet. Exh. S):

> Used to raid pueblos at Galesteo long ago. Raid wagon trains at La Bajada. Apaches hide in bushes along rim.
>
> Jicarillas with leader Julian and 14 lodges of Apaches stayed on hill at the edge of valley below Chilili. Juan with them ten years after big fight at Apache Canyon when many horses killed. Julian and others stole horses at Tajiqui.
>
> Signal from Crow Butte to north Crow Butte—old camping place—camped for piñons in brooks to east, good water there.
>
> Bend near Stanley good place for camp—kill many antelope here in early days. Trail down valley here to Abo and Abo pass. Apaches never go along the Rio Grande. Follow breaks across Estancia to Pecos and Red across to Tecolote. North to Pecos and mountains—go into mountains to gather seed—soldiers never go into mountains—afraid.

Juan's account, recorded by Dr. Hibben, implied there were many expeditions to the east (Pet. Exh. S):

> Trail to Tucumcari Mountain—big trail turns south here to Plaza Larga—big meadows—lots of antelope here—this trail goes to Bosque Redondo and Bosque Largo. Bosque Redondo bad place—many Indians starve there—very bad. Camp of Plains Indians at Plaza Larga—good place for winter—wood, water, good place for hunting—war parties not go that way, not far for buffalo—lots of mesquite beans for grinding up and yucca fruits for mixing with dried meat. Good place for horses used in buffalo hunting. Chief Chino of Jicarilla always camps at Plaza Larga, had many good buffalo horses. Followed down trail to Tucumcari Butte to put hands on the sacred rock there. Then hunted buffalo to east—and winter buffalo south of deep canyon beyond Red River. Brought back much dried meat to camp at Larga.

The Government Evidence

The witnesses for the government generally agreed with the conclusions of witnesses for the tribe, although they differed in details and had less extensive knowledge of the subject.

Dr. Averam B. Bender, historical witness for the government, located the Jicarilla Apaches generally in northeastern New Mexico. On the south he agreed that the southern boundary of the claim ran roughly along the 35th parallel of latitude (a short distance south of Albuquerque). His eastern boundary was quite vague, and he conceded that it ran as far east as the Canadian River and that he had no basis for contesting the claim that it extended on to the 103d parallel of longitude (New Mexico–Texas border). On the west Dr. Bender claimed that the Jicarilla Apache land use and occupancy extended only to the Sangre de Cristo mountains.

Dr. Bender was not a credible witness for the government. His knowledge of the history of the Southwest, particularly New Mexico, was limited to the work he had done in preparation for the case. He testified, based on a report by Governor Charles Bent (the military governor of New Mexico, appointed by General Kearny in 1846), that the territory of the Jicarilla Apaches extended from Pecos to Taos and not beyond the northern border of New Mexico. He did not know that the northeasterly border of New Mexico in 1846 extended to the Arkansas River. The present border was established when it was extended south to the thirty-seventh parallel in 1861.

Dr. Bender had prepared a map that was placed on a panel and presented before the Commission at the hearing in 1959. On this map of New Mexico (showing its present border at the thirty-seventh parallel, not the border as it existed during the period in question), he had shown various locations where he placed Jicarilla Apaches. Testifying before the Commission he was unable to find the locations on his map without the aid of his magnifying glass. (As Bob Harry remarked, "If he put a decal with 'Jicarilla Apache' on his glass he would find Apaches all over his map.")

Plate 18
Robert H. (Bob) Harry
(courtesy Robert H. Harry)

Dr. Bender was questioned by Bob Harry about other sources of his information about American contacts with the Jicarilla Apaches in the years after American occupation of New Mexico. He said that the references to his sources were in his "raw notes," but that he had left these at home. (Bob Harry remarked that "If he cooked his raw notes, they would have been easier to carry to the hearing.") Dr. Bender's testimony, insofar as it was inconsistent with that of Dr. Thomas, was not adopted by the Commission.

The other government witness, Albert T. Schroeder, described the area of traditional land use and occupancy by the Jicarilla Apaches as extending to the Canadian River on the east; to the Sangre de Cristo mountains on the west; along a line north of Taos Pueblo on the north; and along the Pecos, Las Vegas, and Mora line on the south. One dispute between the evidence of Dr. Hibben and Mr. Schroeder's testimony concerning the claim to the central area rose out of the contention originally made by Mr. Schroeder that the Ute Indians occupied a portion of that land, but he eventually conceded that the Utes were not living in New Mexico prior to American occupation.

There was also a contention made by Mr. Schroeder that the eastern portion of the claim area from the Canadian River to the Texas border was used and occupied by the Comanche, Kiowa, and Kiowa Apache Indians, but no evidence was brought forth to sustain the claim of these other Indians, either by their counsel (who was present and attended the hearing) or by the government. In fact Mr. Schroeder conceded that he knew of no evidence to support the claim that the Comanches, Kiowas, and Kiowa Apaches had used and occupied northeastern New Mexico.

Mr. Schroeder also claimed that the Jicarilla Apaches did not hunt east of the Canadian River. He admitted on cross-examination, however, that he had not visited the area east of the Canadian River and that his conclusion was based on nothing more than his own hunches. Mr. Schroeder's testimony generally showed a marked lack of knowledge of the Jicarilla Apache customs and hunting habits.

Dr. Hibben had testified that the Jicarillas used the same hunting camps year after year and that at these same locations they found tipi rings that had been used for years. When Mr. Schroeder was questioned about this testimony on cross-examination and asked if he could express an opinion as to whether or not the Jicarilla Apaches visited the same sites year after year, he stated that "The documents give no statements on that particular phase of Jicarilla life, and nothing as to where their camps were located out on the plains. So, I cannot make any statement one way or another" (59 Tr. 511).

Mr. Schroeder gave contradictory testimony in answer to the question as to whether he had said that the Jicarilla Apaches did not use tipis except in early times (59 Tr. 512):

> **Answer:** That is what Dr. Opler has said. I do not know of any other reference to tipis among the Jicarillas, unless you're going to include the Carlanas who joined them later and lived with them between Taos and Pecos, in that country—they did use the tipi, and probably became part of what is known as the Jicarillas.
>
> **Question:** On that assumption, do you disregard the tipi sites in the area here as Jicarilla sites?
>
> **Answer:** These sites here—have no way of dating them—they may go back to 1700; they may date as early as 1800s, but they have no way of dating them.
>
> **Question:** But that map—they could be dated, couldn't they?
>
> **Answer:** No.
>
> **Question:** You mean these sites cannot be dated by using historical material?
>
> **Answer:** If it's associated and it's a definite type of material that can be restricted to certain given years, yes, it could be dated in that fashion.

Later on he was asked, "You based that conclusion that he cannot identify Indian tribe archaeology just by the tipi rings?" He said that this was his conclusion (59 Tr. 514).

> **Question:** But you do make a definite conclusion that they did not [use tipis].
>
> **Answer:** Well, that is my opinion.
>
> **Question:** You quoted Opler as saying that in early times they probably used the tipis, didn't you?

Answer: He said something along that line, but that is not a direct quote.

Question: The inference is, and I think you also stated, that in American times and since Spanish times, they have not used the tipi. Let me read this—I am calling your attention to *Exhibit S71*, page 3, *Jicarilla Childhood and Truth* by Morris Edward Opler. Mr. Opler was the foremost recognized anthropologist dealing with the Jicarillas was he not?

Answer: Yes, he was.

Question: Let me read this to you, and see if it might change your opinion!

—Jicarilla material life showed unmistakable orientation toward plains culture, as such traits as the parfleche, the tipi, buffalo hunting and travois will indicate. [Schroeder had earlier testified that the Jicarilla Apaches did not use the travois]. Also the warpath and encampments show a distinct decided plains cast. Most of this plains like appearance, however, is somewhat superficial as evidently recent. Though Jicarilla were using the tipi at the time of the American occupation of the region, within the lifetime of the oldest members of the Tribe, the more common and preferred house type was a dome-shaped type frame covered with a thatching of leaves and bark.

Answer: Yes. . . .

Question: Does that coincide with your interpretation? —I don't care who introduced them (the use of the tipi to the Jicarillas), I'm just trying to establish that the Jicarillas used tipis.

Answer: Well, this is strictly on Opler's statement. I don't know how he bases it, but I will go along with Opler's statement.

There are other examples of misquotations by Mr. Schroeder. For example he testified that the Jicarilla Apaches did not hunt east of the Canadian River. He quoted the statement of Juanito

Julian to the effect that the Jicarillas went to the Red (Canadian) River to hunt buffalo. He quoted him as saying: "They did not cross this river for fear of their enemies." This was the basis of his statement that the Jicarillas did not hunt east of the Canadian River.

When questioned about this statement, Mr. Schroeder was asked by the Court to quote directly from the actual testimony he obtained during the deposition of Juanito Julian. The relevant exchange was as follows (59 Tr. 535):

> **Question:** Do you recall how far your father said he went out to hunt the buffalo?
>
> **Answer:** East of the Canadian River.

Mr. Schroeder, recognizing an error, said to the plaintiff's counsel:

> **Question:** I see, I did not paraphrase that correctly there. Is that the point you're getting at?
>
> **Answer:** That is what I'm getting at, yes.
>
> **Question:** Were you so sure that they they didn't go out east of the Canadian that you didn't read that carefully?
>
> **Answer:** Oh well! While I grant you it is an error on my part, I just paraphrased it wrong.
>
> **Question:** Go on down, read some more.

Mr. Schroeder, reading on:

> **Question:** Did he say how far east of the Canadian?
>
> **Question:** Did you recall him saying how many days' journey?
>
> **Answer:** He didn't say.
>
> **Question:** Did your father say they met other Indians out hunting buffalo in the plains?
>
> **Answer:** Well, my father would tell me that the farther

> they would get beyond the Canadian River, the more danger it would be.

Question to Mr. Schroeder, by counsel:

> **Question:** Your statement was, as you say, a paraphrase of this, that they didn't cross the river for fear of their enemies, and that is completely incorrect, isn't it?
>
> **Answer:** That is right. He said the farther they would get beyond the Canadian, the more danger it would be.

There was an obvious contrast between the detailed, first-hand knowledge of Dr. Hibben and Dr. Thomas, based as it was on extensive fieldwork and archival research over a period of years, and the testimony given by Dr. Bender and Mr. Schroeder. Their lack of long-term experience simply made their conclusions untenable, and the Commission evaluated their testimony accordingly.

4

• • •

HISTORICAL EVIDENCE

Dr. Alfred B. Thomas, the Tribe's expert in the history of the claim area, had prepared a study of the Spanish and Mexican periods of New Mexico history applicable to the claim. He had also briefed the Stanford Research Institute reports of governors of New Mexico, Indian agents, and military personnel concerning the Jicarilla Apaches during the period from 1846 to 1887. He was examined on the witness stand by Bob Harry.[2]

Identification of Apache Bands

Among the ancestors of the Jicarilla Apache Tribe were numerous bands of Indians known to the Spaniards by various names. The Querechos and Vaqueros were identified by the chroniclers of the Coronado expedition and are considered to be the ancestors of the Jicarillas. The Penxaye Apaches were encountered by Captain Juan de Ulibarrí in 1706, from the Raton Mountains to the Arkansas River; Antonio Valverde encountered the Carlana Apaches on the eastern slope of the mountains in Colorado and the Quartalejo Apaches in eastern Colorado and western Kansas.

Governor Thomas Vélez Cachupín identified the Palomas, the Jicarillas, the Carlanas, and the Chipaynes in the Taos-Pecos area in the early eighteenth century. The Achos, Rio Colorados, and Conejeros were reported in or east of the Sangre de Cristos in the early eighteenth century. In the eastern part of New Mexico along the Canadian River were the Chipaynes and the Lemitas or Nementinas.

The government witness, Mr. Schroeder, agreed with Dr. Thomas that after 1750 all of these bands and groups were referred to by the Spaniards as Jicarillas. Band names were derived from the places where they lived, their leaders, or some other outstanding characteristic.

In modern times these bands were organized into two divisions, each consisting of approximately six bands, one division generally operating east of the Rio Grande and the other generally operating west of the river.

The eastern group was known as the Llanero, or Plains, People, and the other group was known as the Ollero, or Mountain, People, living generally in the mountain areas of northern New Mexico. These divisions and the bands within them were united by a common dialect, a common religion, and a common culture. They became a cohesive tribe in the late eighteenth and early nineteenth centuries under the influence of the Plains Indians and the pressure of the American occupation. The bands joined together and became a "tribe" in the legal sense when they were finally placed on the present reservation in 1887; then the distinct bands were no longer able to travel and hunt as seperate groups. At that time they were recognized by the United States government as a "tribe."

The Spanish Period, 1541–1821

From the beginning of recorded history in the Southwest, chronicled by early explorers, missionaries, colonizers, and military authorities, the Jicarilla Apaches and their ancestors were consistently found throughout the claim area and were using and occupying all of the claim-area lands according to their Indian way of life.

Coronado encountered Apaches in 1541 on an expedition eastward from New Mexico. In 1598 Governor Juan de Oñate assigned missionaries to "the Apaches from the Sierra Nevada toward the north and east and the province of Taos." In the same year, Mendoza met Apaches between Pecos and present-day Tucumcari, near the Canadian River, and used them as guides.

The Spaniards reported, "We found rancherías inhabitated by people of the Apache nations who were masters of these plains." The Spanish reported that from the earliest day, the Apaches had close relations with the Pueblo Indians—particularly those of Pecos, Picuris, and Taos—visiting, trading, and hunting with them. In 1686 Father Alonzo Posada regularly reported on the Apache nation, stating that this nation dwelled along the eastern frontier and continued along the Sierra Blanca, which extends from east to west and is the closest range on the northern side of New Mexico.

In July 1696 Don Diego de Vargas, during the reconquest of New Mexico following the Pueblo Rebellion of 1680, marched north from Taos into the present San Luis Valley of southern Colorado, where he found the Acho Apaches along the banks of the Culebra River.

All of these Apache groups encountered by the Spaniards were identified by all of the authorities as the ancestors of the Jicarilla Apaches.

The expedition of Ulibarrí in 1706 encountered bands of Conejero, Acho, and Rio Colorado Apaches beyond Cimarron Creek and bands called Flecha de Palo and Carlana at the foot of the Raton Mountains and east of the Sierra Blanca. In the canyon of the Purgatoire River, and later along the Arkansas River, he met Indians of the Penxaye Band of Apaches.

As Ulibarrí traveled east from present-day Pueblo, Colorado, he encountered the rancherías of the Apaches of El Cuartelejo. They occupied an extensive region that included the area from present-day Kiowa County (in eastern Colorado) to Scott County, Kansas, and as far north as the South Platte River.

In 1719 the Valverde expedition left Taos to make war against the Utes and Comanches. The Jicarilla Apaches were encountered near present-day Cimarron, New Mexico, and the expedition was guided by the Apaches' Chief Carlana along the Purgatoire and Arkansas rivers. Cuartelejo Apaches numbering more than a thousand were encountered, as well as bands of Calchufine and Paloma Apaches—all identified by the authorities as ancestors to the present-day Jicarilla Apaches.

Captain Pedro de Villasur's expedition in 1720 was sent beyond El Cuartelejo, to locate the French. Although most of the expedition was destroyed by the Pawnees in present-day Kansas, the reports of the expedition confirmed that the same Apache bands occupied the territory as far east as Kansas and as far north as the Platte River.

The vast extent of the lands occupied by Jicarilla Apaches is demonstrated by the records of the Spanish Governor Juan Domingo de Bustamante during 1723, when he reported that the Jicarilla Apache lands extended to the Pawnee lands in the northeast and those of other tribes in Kansas and Texas.

In 1733 the Spanish established a mission for Jicarilla Apaches 10 miles north of Taos; Apaches accepted baptism and were friendly to the Spaniards. The Spaniards accepted them as guides throughout the claim area.

In the latter part of the eighteenth century, the reports of the Spanish indicated that the Jicarilla Apaches continued to occupy their ancestral lands. Governor Cachupín's report to the viceroy in September 1752 stated that during the winter, men of the Apache, Carlana, Paloma, and Cuartelejo bands had been in the environs of Pecos with their families, and that they were accustomed to go to the plains to hunt buffalo for their support. He further stated that the Spanish used the Apaches as spies against the Comanches, and that they were able to reconnoiter for one hundred leagues because of their extensive knowledge of the land.

Again in 1754, Governor Cachupín reported that the various bands of Apaches lived as far as the boundaries of Texas, and that they maintained peaceful relations with the Spanish. He further indicated that they remained in the neighborhood of the Pecos, except when they went back and forth to the plains to see their relatives.

In 1763, when Spain acquired the Louisiana Territory by transfer from France, the Spanish authorities organized the northern frontier of the empire to meet the possibility of attacks. The Marqués de Rubí made an extensive inspection of the northern frontier, and in a report dated April 10, 1768, he enclosed a map of this frontier drawn by his engineer, Nicolás de La Fora. This map placed the Apaches east of the Pecos, extending well into western Texas.

The Escalante expedition of 1776, directed toward the Pacific Ocean, located bands of the Southern Utes to the west of the Continental Divide, entirely outside the claim area.

Governor El Caballero de Croix reported for the years 1771–81 that troops and settlers of New Mexico, with the aid of the Utes and Jicarilla Apaches, punished the Comanches and that the Comanches had been unable to resist the New Mexico forces.

The ultimate defeat of the Comanches in New Mexico was the result of work of Governor Juan Bautista de Anza, who took office in New Mexico in 1777. He made an alliance with the Utes and the Jicarillas, and in 1779, using his new allies as guides, he marched north from Taos to the San Luis Valley of southern Colorado, thence eastward past Pike's Peak and across the Front Range of the Rockies into the eastern plains. After the guides located the Comanches, Anza killed their famous chief Cuerno Verde in a battle near Pueblo, forcing the Comanches to seek peace. During the latter part of his campaign he used only Jicarilla guides (because the Utes departed the expedition to return to their own lands southwest of Cochetopa Pass).

The treaty of peace between Anza and the Comanches in 1786 recognized the territory of the Jicarillas east of Pecos in providing safe passage for the Comanches to trade with the Pueblos. The Comanches agreed to keep peace with all Indians who were friends with the Spaniards.

Governor Fernando de la Concha reported in 1794 that the Jicarillas were living between Pecos and Taos, hunting buffalo in the east, sowing their lands, harvesting their crops, and maintaining their agreements. At the same time, Cordero located the territory of the Jicarilla Apaches as extending north to the thirty-eighth parallel.

Hernando Cortez reported in 1799 that the Jicarillas occupied the great plains and sands between Pecos and the left bank of the Rio Grande and lived in the limits of the province, which then extended beyond the Arkansas River. A map by López at the end of the century showed the Jicarilla Apaches occupying all of eastern New Mexico. An earlier map by H. Jaillot, the famous French cartographer, showed Apaches occupying all of northeastern New Mexico as the territory existed at that time (maps 2–3).

The peaceful relations between the Jicarilla Apaches, Comanches, and other Plains tribes established by Governor Anza and his successors were disrupted by the transfer of the Louisiana Territory from France to the United States in 1803, a short time after Spain had reconveyed that area to France.

From 1803 to 1821, when the Adams-Onis Treaty was ratified, no one was sure where the boundary between the Louisiana Territory and Spain's possessions would be placed. Spain was fearful of American plans in the Southwest and sent out frequent patrols from New Mexico which went as far as 500 miles eastward along the Canadian River, northeast as far as the Pawnee villages, and north to the mouth of the Yellowstone River.

Spain's difficulties at home and in Mexico, coupled with its growing conflicts with the United States, produced a lack of interest in the affairs of the Indians, so that reports concerning the Indians to the north and east in New Mexico are almost nonexistent for this period. A lack of knowledge and interest on the part of the officials of the United States combined to produce a minimum of reliable reports on the American side also.

Among the meager accounts of the period, there was one that came from a hunt in 1809 by a combined party of Utes and Jicarilla Apaches, which had assembled at San Antonio Peak, south of the Conejos River on the Colorado–New Mexico border. They traveled over the Front Range of the Rockies and then into the plains, where a battle was fought with a combined force of Kiowa and Comanche Indians.

In 1819 Lieutenant Arze made a reconnaissance that included the San Luis Valley, the Front Range of the Rockies around Pike's Peak, and on along the Arkansas River. He located the Jicarilla Apaches in the San Juan Mountains, west of the San Luis Valley. His report went on to state that he actually encountered no other Indian tribes, nor did he meet any Americans.

The reports of the Spanish officials in the later part of the eighteenth century established the location of the Jicarilla Apaches as well as the range of adjoining tribes. Thus it had been established that a body of the Jicarillas was living between Pecos and Taos and hunting to the east, while other bands occupied the area as far north as the Arkansas, and yet another large band was permanently located west of the Rio Grande, in the region of the Conejos River.

A consistent pattern of buffalo hunting on the eastern limits of the territory was maintained throughout the period. It was further established by the reports of Anza and others that there were no permanent Ute settlements within the claim area, and that the Comanche encroachments on Apache lands in New Mexico and Colorado had ceased as the result of the treaty concluded by Governor Anza in 1786.

The Mexican Period, 1821–1846

From 1821 to 1846, the claim area south of the Arkansas River was under the jurisdiction of Mexico. Political domination by Mexico was weak and loose, however, and the area was substantially under the control of its Indian inhabitants during this period.

There were no official Mexican reports on the Indians. Reports of Indian activity were scarce from American sources as well; generally these reports were only of contacts along the Arkansas River and along the eastern boundary of the Jicarilla Apache claim area, the routes generally used by traders during the period.

American and French traders began to penetrate New Mexico for commercial purposes after the Mexican Revolution (1821). These traders brought Plains Indians into the area along the Arkansas to trap and hunt. Licenses to American traders were granted by William Clark, territorial governor of Missouri, and others. The rights extended to the headwaters of the Arkansas and Platte rivers.

American expeditions also made explorations through part of the territory to study the Louisiana Purchase country. Lieutenant Zebulon Pike made his expedition in 1806. He was followed by the expeditions of Long in 1820, Fowler in 1821, and Sibley in 1825.

These expeditions encountered few Indians of any tribe within the claim area. Fowler did report that he was visited by a delegation of Jicarilla Apaches, on the Culebra River in Colorado, who threatened to steal his horses.

Pike and Long, as well as Lewis and Clark, were confused by the Spanish and French names of the different tribes encountered along the Arkansas and Platte rivers. The Lewis and Clark Expedition mentioned the "Paducar," and Long encountered "Paduoca." Fowler mentioned the Kiowa "Paduce" and "Padduce," who he said were not Comanches. Many of these American explorers identified the Paducas with the Apaches; Secoy specifically identified the Paducas as Apaches. Confusion in the identification of these tribes by early American explorers may well have resulted in the failure to recognize the presence of the Jicarilla Apaches in New Mexico.

Colonel Dodge, on a reconnaissance of the Rocky Mountains in 1835, reported that a tribe of Apaches called "Apaches of the Plains," numbering about twelve hundred, frequented the Arkansas and Platte rivers near the mountains, for the purpose of killing buffalo. Dr. George B. Grinnell would later identify these Plains or Prairie Apaches as "Jicarillas."

Just before the American occupation in New Mexico, the Jicarilla Apaches were reported to be living in the claim area by others. In 1845 Lieutenant J. W. Abert encountered a band of Jicarilla Apaches on the Purgatoire River, a short distance from Bent's Fort. Lieutenant W. H. Emery reported Apaches to the west of the Rio Del Norte; another band was reported to the east and yet another band on the "Purgatory Mountain," and he stated that the Apaches near Taos were the same stock as those he had met.

Although the Jicarilla Apaches had gradually withdrawn from the northeastern limits of the claim area, under pressure from the Americans, and they avoided the regularly traveled routes of traders and military expeditions, they continued to use and occupy substantially all of the claim area for their agriculture, hunting, and gathering activities up to the date of the American occupation of New Mexico in 1846 and thereafter.

The American Period

New Mexico became United States territory on August 18, 1846, following the occupation of Santa Fe by American troops under the command of General Stephen Watts Kearny. The peace treaty between the United States and Mexico, the Treaty of Guadalupe Hidalgo, was signed on February 2, 1848, and ratified shortly thereafter by the Senate of the United States. Colonel John M. Washington was appointed military commander and provisional governor of New Mexico, arriving in Santa Fe on October 10, 1848.

One of the duties specifically enjoined upon Washington was the protection of the inhabitants of New Mexico against Indian incursions and the defense of the territory from invasion. James S. Calhoun was appointed the first Indian agent in New Mexico in 1849. After his arrival in July of that year, he reported to the commissioner of Indian affairs that the wild Indians had been particularly hostile and aggressive, having raided the settlements, stolen livestock, and wantonly murdered the settlers.

The military seemed powerless to prevent these raids, and the settlers were critical, claiming that the soldiers were incapable of defending the settlements and that they were afraid to follow the Indians to their hideouts. Colonel Washington held a council with leaders of some of the Jicarilla Apache bands, including a band near Abiquiu, and "made a peace" with them; this "peace" did not last beyond the spring of the year.

A number of contacts were reported with the Jicarilla Apaches, and several American military expeditions were undertaken against these Indians throughout the northern portions of the territory during the period between 1845 and 1848.

In 1845 Lieutenant J. W. Abert encountered a band of Jicarilla Apaches on the Purgatoire River, a short distance south of Bent's Fort. The same band was reported by Colonel W. H. Emery in 1846. Orville Pratte, a trader, reported the presence of five hundred Apaches at Abiquiu, west of the Rio Grande, in August 1848. In July 1848 Major W. W. Reynolds pursued a large band of Jicarilla Apaches into the San Juan Mountains of Colorado, northwest of the Taos Valley.

Captain Charles Williams encountered a village camp of Jicarilla Apaches in the San Juan Mountains, sixty miles northwest of Taos, in November 1848. In that same month, Lieutenant Whittlesey received a report of Apache activity on the Purgatoire River of Colorado, but was unable to reach that area from Taos because of heavy snows. In December 1848 Major Beall made a reconnaissance eastward from Taos to Point of Rocks, then northwesterly along the Raton Mountains to the western mountains of Colorado, checking on rumors of Apache activity in that area.

Returning to Taos through Sangre de Cristo Pass (Colorado), Major Beall found a village of Jicarilla Apaches located on Indian Creek, at the western entrance to the pass. He learned from these Apaches that a second band of this group was on the Canadian River in the southeastern part of the claim; a third band was located on the Ojo Caliente River in the southwestern part of the claim. A few months later, Sergeant Bally met with Jicarilla Apache chiefs at Santa Barbara, about 20 miles south of Taos.

Then in May 1849, Captain Chapman pursued Jicarillas southwest of Abiquiu and destroyed a village, killing about twenty of the several hundred Indians encountered. In August 1849 a band of Jicarilla Apaches camped near Las Vegas for trading purposes was attacked and scattered by Captain Henry

M. Judd. Other attacks were made on Jicarilla Apache bands throughout an area ranging from 19 to 43 miles southeast of Las Vegas, in the direction of the Bosque Redondo.

A major incident occurred in November 1849, when Captain Greer conducted an expedition against Jicarilla Apaches who were reported to have killed some of the White family near Point of Rocks in northeastern New Mexico and to have imprisoned Mrs. White, her child, and a servant. Greer trailed this band of Apaches from Point of Rocks by way of Palo Blanco Creek to their camp south of Tucumcari, where his troops killed many of the Indians in a running fight over 22 miles, scattering the rest into the surrounding area.

When Indian Agent Calhoun arrived in New Mexico, he had no prior knowledge or experience in dealing with Indians, and the Department of Indian Affairs in Washington was unable to give him any help. Commissioner of Indian Affairs William Medill wrote that so little was known of the condition and situation of the Indians in the region that no specific instructions relative to them could be given.

Calhoun was directed to gather statistical and other information that would give the department an understanding of the Indian situation. Superintendent Mitchell in St. Louis reported that the boundaries dividing the different tribes had never been settled or defined, and that once they were clearly understood, each tribe could be held responsible for any depredations that might be committed within their respective territories. Agent Calhoun, in attempting to determine the boundaries of the Indian tribes in New Mexico, submitted a sketch map in 1849 to the commissioner and another map on March 20, 1850 showing his findings. With the 1850 map, he attached a report, also dated March 20, 1850, in which he stated (in part):

> You will notice on the returned map that I have marked, with some approach to accuracy, seven counties of this territory, as organized. The four great tribes, the Apaches, Comanches, Navajos, and Utahs, make frequent excursions into these counties.
>
> All east, west, north and south of the outer lead and red-ink

> lines is regarded as Indian country. On the east side of the Arkansas, the Arapahoes, Cheyennes, Kiowas and other roaming Indians are to be found. These Indians are frequently on the west side of said river, hunting, trading and uniting with the Indians of this territory in their wars and robberies against the people of the United States and Mexico.
>
> The apparent dividing line between the Apaches and the Utahs commences on the Rio Del Norte, about latitude 37° [present northern boundary of New Mexico]. The land northeast and east of this point between the pencil and red-ink lines, to the Arkansas is accorded to the Jicarillas. Occasionally, every tribe of Indians is to be found in this region.
>
> East and south of said lead and red-ink lines, the Apaches first, and then the Comanches, are found. I have no means of ascertaining the supposed dividing line between these tribes. The Comanches are chiefly south of the Apache district, east of the Rio Del Norte, and between it and the State of Texas.
>
> The strip of country running south from the county of San Miguel Del Bado, known as the Apache country, is not less than 300 miles wide. Not an inch of Comanche country is to be found on the returned map, although I have written upon an outer edge the word "Comanches," for the purpose of showing the direction of their localities.
>
> You will perceive, upon the map as marked, there is but very little of the Navajo country, less of the Utahs, and none whatever of the Comanches, but an immense strip claimed by the Apaches.

On August 9, 1851, Calhoun was appointed the first civil governor of the New Mexico territory. He also continued to serve as Indian agent until the end of his term.

Calhoun's peace efforts were interrupted by minor difficulties with the "wild" Indian tribes and some troubles with the Mexicans, but finally his efforts culminated in a treaty with the

"Apaches east of the Rio Del Norte" on April 2, 1851. This was the only treaty of many with the Apaches that was ratified by the Senate. It was not a treaty of cession, as no land was involved.

Governor Calhoun became seriously ill in April 1852. He assigned his duties as Indian agent to John Greiner at the end of that month and made preparations to return to the East. He died somewhere on the plains, before reaching Missouri.

Greiner, as agent, wrote on March 30, 1852, to the commissioner:

> The northern Apaches—from their location, and their eminent knowledge of the country, have the power of cutting off all communication between us and the states, if they choose—and as they range through all the northern settlements and hold daily intercourse with the people—they could be made to feel that it is in their interest to remain at peace.
>
> The northern Apaches have never received anything from our government (with exception of a few presents given them by the agents at Taos and Antoine Chico,) and mischievous persons have taunted them by saying that the Navajos and Utahs, have received large appropriations.
>
> A number of Jicarillas met with the governor and superintendent of Indian Affairs at Pecos on Saturday, the 20th of March 1852 to hold a council. [Chiefs] Chacon, Lobo, San Pablo and San Antonio, the captains of the four principal bands, were present, and about 100 warriors representing all of the Jicarillas. The greatest harmony prevailed in the council. They expressed themselves highly gratified to see us come among them without arms, and without an escort as it showed our confidence in them.
>
> They had suffered much from the depredations of the Arapahoes who had killed some of their people and stolen their horses—Governor William Carr Lane succeeded Governor Calhoun, and he evolved a policy of keeping the New Mexico Indians quiet by giving them rations, believing

> this was a better method of fighting. He made agreements with the Apaches in the southwest and northeast, including the Jicarillas, in which he agreed to give them rations for five years and additional aid, provided they would work.
>
> A number of the Jicarillas in the northeast were induced to settle on farms west of the Rio Grande on the Rio Puerco. Governor Lane expended about $20,000 in the execution of this policy. When his treaties were not approved and the food supply cut off, the Jicarillas became destitute and began to plunder the cattle herds of the settlers for food.
>
> As a result, the army again was called upon to take the field against the Jicarillas in 1854 and 1855. Acting Governor [William S.] Messervy reported in March 1854 that the Jicarillas either had to steal or starve, since the government had not carried out its agreements. What amounted to a declaration of war was initiated against the Jicarillas. Governor Messervy reported the depredations had been continued since September of the previous year, growing more frequent from month to month, and resulted in the loss of property, the aggregate value of $50–100,000 and many valuable lives.
>
> This conduct induced a Major Blake of the U.S. Army to send out Lieutenant [John W.] Davidson with a party of dragoons to watch and restrain their movements. When this party was seen by the Indians, a battle ensued which resulted in the loss of 24 dragoons killed, and 23 wounded. The loss on the part of the Indians was not ascertained.

Shortly after this occurrence, the acting governor and superintendent of Indian affairs in the territory, David Meriwether, issued a proclamation declaring that war existed between the United States and the Jicarilla Apache Tribe of Indians and all their aiders and abettors; a formal peace treaty was never signed by the government or ratified by Congress (technically a state of war still exists between the Jicarilla Apache Tribe and the United States). The Indians sued for peace. Meriwether wrote:

> The Indians have already sent in a delegation to sue for peace as before stated, in the daily expectation of hearing from them again. When peace be made, it will be impossible for the Indians to refrain from stealing . . . without subsistence and provisions such as corn and beef . . . on the part of the United States . . .

Governor Meriwether's statement of the Jicarilla Apache claim is interesting:

> The Jicarilla Apaches formerly occupied the eastern portion of the territory, extending from the Rio Grande eastward beyond the Red River between the 34th and 37th parallels of north latitude, but were removed and located by my predecessor west of the Rio Grande. A part of this band under their Chief Francisco Chacon, were assembled and fed around a farm in the vicinity of Abiquiu during the spring and summer of 1853, under the compact heretofore alluded to, but the farm yielded but little produce.
>
> The Jicarillas now claim a region of country of infinite space, lying west of the Rio Grande, and the head of the Chama and Puerco Rivers, but they roam over many other portions of the territory. It is confidently believed that no other single band of Indians have committed an equal amount of depredation upon, and caused so much trouble and annoyance to people of this territory, as the Jicarilla Tribe. They are supposed to number about 150 warriors and probably 500 souls; they own a large number of horses and mules; and whenever there is mischief brewing, they invariably have a hand in it.

Military dispatches in 1854 evidenced the wide range of territory encompassing the range of the Jicarilla Apaches—some excerpts cited were:

> March 8, 1854 at Mesa Rica between soldiers of Fort Union and Jicarillas.
>
> Apaches at Guadalupita (southeast of Las Vegas) [dispatch of March 8, 1854].

> Apache attacked between Ocate and "El Corral de los Apaches" [March 8, 1854].
>
> Jicarilla Apaches—two chiefs at Cantonment Burgwin (Taos) friendly talk [Kit Carson, March 27, 1854].
>
> Hundred warriors, Jicarillas, with their families near Picuris (between Santa Fe and Taos) [Carson].
>
> Bell's fight east of the Canadian, in which Lobo was killed [General Garland, March 29, 1854].
>
> Major Thompson demands Jicarilla Apaches deliver four members as hostages to Canton Burgwin—alarmed they fled, soldiers pursued and a fight occurred, in which the troops were worsted [Messervy, March 31, 1854].
>
> March 30, 1854, Lieutenant Davidson's command defeated by Jicarilla Apaches at Embudo Mountains (on Rio Grande between Santa Fe and Taos) [Carson, April 2, 1854].
>
> Jicarilla Apaches leave El Rito from mountains of Ojo Caliente [Head agent, April 7, 1854].
>
> Whole tribe of Jicarilla Apaches at war [Head agent, April 7, 1854].
>
> Chacon's band on Rio San Antonio (near Conejos, Colorado) [Head agent, April 7, 1854].
>
> Battle of San Juan Mountains (head of Vallecitos) through the San Juan Mountains from April 8 through April 12, 1854 [Cooke, May 24, 1854].

A portion of a dispatch from Colonel Lieutenant Colonel Philip St. George Cooke described the ferocity of the battles against the Jicarilla Apaches in 1854 as follows:

> Very early in the night—the pursuit was renewed. I found after some miles that the enemy's horse tracks converged in the snow on a mountainside—there had been broken a path two feet deep which led over the great obstacles of a forest of aspens and pines prostrated by storm—through bogs where mules had to be unpacked, up and down steep

> mountainsides from whose summits—a world of blank snows spread unlimited to the west; over a stream half-bridged with ice and deep snow, where the horses fell and every mule had to be unpacked—American horses, two in file, first broke the path of this retreat. Such was a scene of the enemies' flight by moonlight—the tracks of bare and diminutive feet left a feeble memorial of its sufferings—
>
> Many dead horses—some of them had been butchered—marked their retreat; and signal smokes now in several directions—and other signs indicated now that the hard pressed tribe had divided and sought temporary retreats in the rocky and lofty mountains everywhere to be seen.

The chase ended on the headwaters of the Chama River. Jicarilla men, women, and children were killed, drowned, frozen, or simply disappeared.

In May a band of Jicarillas consisting of thirty lodges crossed the Rio Grande northwest of Fort Massachusetts (near present Fort Garland, Colorado). They were pursued by General James H. Carlton through Mosca and Sangre de Cristo passes eastward into the Raton Mountains.

In January 1855 Kit Carson reported that Jicarilla Apaches had attacked Pueblo, Colorado, killing fourteen and wounding two, and had carried off a woman and two children as captives. Carson further reported that "a party, consisting mostly of Jicarilla Apaches and Utes, reside between Taos and Salt Lake; Blanca, who is said to have headed the party, I've never seen nor does he come often about our settlements unless when he intends mischief."

In March of 1855, Colonel Thomas T. Fauntleroy with a force of five hundred men overtook a hundred lodges of Jicarilla Apaches and Utes in Saguache (Cochitopa Pass), about 120 miles northwest of Fort Massachusetts. After an all-day battle, the Utes and Apaches separated. The Utes crossed the mountains to the southwest and were thereafter ignored by Colonel Fauntleroy, who continued to pursue the Jicarillas retreating to the northeast.

The pursuit passed through Poncha Pass, across the Arkansas River, and northeastward between the dividing waters of the Arkansas River and Valles Salados (South Park), forcing the Jicarillas to scatter among the mountains west of Pike's Peak. Fauntleroy then turned south, encountered and attacked another band of Apaches on the Arkansas River, and returned to Fort Massachusetts by way of the Wet Mountains and Mosca Pass. Agent Carson reported that this was one of the most effective campaigns made against the Jicarilla Apaches.

In a number of separate campaigns during the months of May through July 1855, Colonels Ceran St. Vrain and Fauntleroy hunted down the Jicarilla Apaches through the Raton, Sangre de Cristo, and Wet mountains of Colorado as far as Hardscrabble Creek, until all organized resistance in that area ceased. These campaigns put an end for all time to such resistance on the part of the Jicarilla Apache Tribe.

In August of 1855, Governor Meriwether was designated by the president to negotiate "Articles of Convention under the appropriation of $30,000 with the Apache, Navajo, Utah Indians in New Mexico by which permanent and well defined relations of amity shall be established between them and the United States." The treaty was signed at Abiquiu on September 10, 1855. The Jicarillas agreed to cede all claims to lands in New Mexico except what was to be reserved to them, and the United States agreed to make certain payments. The treaty agreed to set aside to the Jicarilla Apaches a reservation running from the source of Cebolla Creek (emptying into the Chama) and west of the Continental Divide, then south along the Continental Divide to the mountains that divide the waters of the Chama from the Rio Puerco, then along the dividing line of the mountains eastward to the headwaters of the Arroyo Puerto de Bajo, then down the creek to its entrance into the Chama River, then to the place of the beginning.

The United States also agreed to pay $3,000 each year in 1856, 1857, and 1858; $2,000 for the next two succeeding years; and $1,000 for the next twenty years beginning in 1862. The government reserved the right to determine the allocation of the annual payments, whether as money, educational contributions, or other benefits.

Almost immediately after the treaty had been signed, settlers claimed rights to the land that was to be given to the Jicarilla Apaches as a reservation, and as a result the treaty was not ratified by the Senate.

Prior to the treaties, rationing agencies were established in 1853 in Abiquiu and Taos for the Muache Utes and Jicarilla Apaches. The Jicarillas continued to hunt and gather, but most of them also drew rations at those agencies. Agent Carson wrote in July 1858 that the greater part of the Jicarilla Apaches were on the east side of the Rio Del Norte (Rio Grande) and that they were providing for their own maintenance with the assistance given them by the inhabitants, who bought their pots and baskets and paid them for their labor.

Carson further stated that they did not trouble him much for food; they went to the Spanish Peaks and east of the mountains to hunt. They returned loaded with meat, having enough left over to sell. He further reported it was impractical to commence the practice of monthly ration issues, since the Indians were scattered in different parts of the country, and he had done all in his power to keep them in small bands, so that by their hunting they could assist in their maintenance and reduce the cost of supporting them. He went on to state that he thought the Jicarillas should be attached to the Taos agency, because they would be better able to provide for their own maintenance. In August of 1860, Carson reported some 950 Jicarilla living in the vicinity of the agency, "living by the chase."

When Confederate forces invaded New Mexico in 1861 and occupied Santa Fe, various hunting tribes, including the Jicarilla Apaches, were left without restraint by the Indian agencies and the military. James L. Collins, superintendent of Indian affairs in Santa Fe, wrote on October 8, 1861:

> Within the district thus occupied by the invaders are included all the Apache tribes of Indian tribes except the

> Jicarillas. The Agents for these Indians have been driven from their agencies, and the Indians, being left without restraint, are overrunning the country, and committing depredations wherever it suits their inclination or convenience.

On September 10, 1861, the Cimarron agency was established. From here, on this date, "yearly presents" were dispensed to the Indians, according to Indian Agent Arny. He stated that they were removed from the temptations to which they were exposed at Taos; that is from the use of intoxicating liquors. They expressed themselves as satisfied with the presents they received, except that they were short of materials for building lodges, and they wanted more of such supplies. On September 24, 1861, Arny wrote:

> The Mohuache Tribe of Utahs and the Jicarilla Apaches possess the balance of power in the Territory of New Mexico. They stand between the unfriendly Indian and the citizens, and if they were to array themselves against the citizens, there would be no security for life or property here, unless at great expense to the general government to sustain an army to keep them in subjection.

The Indian agents recognized that it was impossible to restrain the Jicarilla Apaches from roaming over the territory without a reservation and without adequate rations to sustain them. Superintendent Collins wrote in October 1861 as follows:

> More than a year ago, I attempted to demonstrate to you the absurdity of supposing that the Superintendent of Indian affairs, with one or two Agents, could prevent the Utah and Apache tribes of Indians from ranging over the country—a right that seems to have been conceded to them ever since the country has been occupied by the whites. According to my knowledge of history the Government of Spain never attempted to prohibit either of these tribes from passing over the country in any and every direction that suited their own purposes and convenience. The same privileges were allowed to them by the Government of

> Mexico: and up to the present time no change has been made or attempted to be made, in this respect, by the United States.
>
> That there is a necessity for a change of this kind, no one I suppose will pretend to deny, but it can only be accomplished by an Act of Congress and forced in the main by the military power of the Government.
>
> The Government of the United States has, from its first establishment, recognized the proprietary right in the Indian to all of the land, which he has been found occupying, and has only divested him with that right by a formal treaty and the payment of an equivalent in money. Nothing of this kind has ever been done with the Utahs and Apaches, consequently their right of occupation is yet recognized by the Government and even if it were possible for the Agents to deprive them of the enjoyment of this right, which you very well know is out of their power to do, an attempt to do it would be an unwarranted assumption of authority on their part.

Agent Arny expressed similar views on January 6, 1862:

> My opinion is that Treaties should be made with all the Indians in New Mexico and also with the Confederate Tribes in Colorado requiring each tribe to cultivate peaceful relations with all other Indians and binding them to cease hostilities with all tribes who are at peace with the Government of the United States.
>
> The treaties should be made with the Indians of New Mexico to obtain from them the right they claim to roam where they please in that Territory. That in consideration for the relinquishment of this right they receive a certain specified tract of land as their reservation the boundaries of which should be definitely defined and the Indians required to remain on it being furnished with the necessary farming implements for its cultivation and the Whites and Mexicans excluded therefrom unless by permit of the agent.

In the latter 1860s, some Jicarilla Apache bands continued

to live on both the east and the west sides of the Rio Grande. Thirty-nine lodges of over two hundred Indians were reported camped near Abiquiu in 1867; some of them had not been in Cimarron for more than five years. Collins reported that the Jicarilla Apaches were composed of twelve bands, two of which were west of the Rio Grande, and that they were the most advanced of the "wild" tribes of New Mexico. The following is an excerpt from a report Agent Arny wrote in 1867:

> The Utahs and Apaches of Cimarron have also remained quiet and peaceable, committing no depredations whatever that have been reported to their agent—these Indians had been fed by the military ever since last September because ex-commissioner Cooley forbade their being fed by the Indian Department to the extent of $500 a month, as I had authorized, and upon his disapproval of my action I stopped feeding, and they began to steal.
>
> General Carlton saying (which is a fact) 'that it was cheaper to feed than it is to fight them,' authorized their being fed over $3,000 a month instead of $500 a month which gave satisfaction at that time.
>
> I would respectfully recommend, in behalf of these Indians, the purchase of the Maxwell Grant, and then they could be made in less than one year self-sustaining. There is no use in avoiding the issue. It is useless to talk of moving them elsewhere; they would resist to the last extremity.

Agent Arny continued to report that the Jicarilla Apaches roamed both east and west of the Rio Grande wherever they pleased, and that they could not be controlled. He persisted in arguing for a reservation between the Navajo River and the San Juan River, "in the valley east of the proposed Utah Reservation." In 1871 many of the Apache bands continued to hunt in their traditional areas. Ruedel, the agent at Cimarron, wrote in May 1871:

> San Pablo, an Apache Chief, told me—last March, that he should take his people to Colorado to hunt, they should be

> absent during three full moons and return—about the beginning of July—José Largo, another Apache chief was at Red River with his band—Chino with his people—was going to join José Largo—no complaints against him in the papers of this [New Mexico] or Colorado territory.

In 1870 the English company that purchased the Maxwell Land Grant stated its intention to force the Jicarilla Apaches off the land. Agent Wilson wrote on September 1, 1870:

> They are a great deal dissatisfied over the sale of "Maxwell Grant" to the English Company, they insisting they own the land, and they only allowed Maxwell to live on it because he was their friend. The new company are anxious to get them off the land. This may possibly lead to trouble.

Three months later, on December 6, 1870, Agent E. B. Dennison, reporting from Cimarron, wrote:

> They [the Jicarillas] had so long held this section as their home, as a resting place, retreating to it as a point of safety if punished in war with their enemies the Indians of the plains, most of them were born here, their ancestors for years past have been buried here, they entertain heathenist superstitions, they hold these valleys sacred, here they make medicine, hold their feasts, perform their ceremonials of lamentations for their dead—

As a result of the pressure to get the Indians off the Maxwell Grant, a treaty was signed between the United States and the principal Jicarilla Apache chiefs that provided for a reservation for the Jicarillas in northwestern New Mexico, adjoining the Navajo on the west and the Ute reservation on the north. The United States agreed to pay over a period of years, and the Jicarillas agreed to surrender all claims to their land. This treaty, like that of 1855, was not ratified.

The Jicarillas stayed at the Cimarron agency, from where they continued their annual hunting activities. Although the agency was abolished on September 30, 1876, the Jicarillas continued to maintain their "headquarters" there. Because of the abolition of the agency, scanty provisions were supplied for them, and their subsistence continued to be obtained in the usual way, by hunting throughout northeastern New Mexico.

Attempts were made to move the Jicarillas to Fort Stanton on the Mescalero Reservation in 1878, but the Jicarillas objected to "being jumped around about like grasshoppers." They persistently refused to go to the Mescalero Reservation; after three years of effort, the government finally succeeded in moving only thirty-two Jicarilla Apaches out of a total of nine hundred from Cimarron to Fort Stanton.

In 1880 authorities in Washington and Santa Fe succeeded in securing a reservation for them at the location of what is now their present reservation in northwestern New Mexico. Hardly had the Indians become established there when powerful interests (settlers and stockmen) once again forced their removal to the Mescalero Reservation.

The reservation in northwest New Mexico was set aside by executive order on September 21, 1881, but in 1883 a sum of $5,000 was allocated to be used to remove the Jicarillas to the Mescalero Reservation. The early reservation was abandoned to the squatters, distribution of supplies and food was stopped, and a route of travel to the Mescalero area was planned.

The Jicarillas were bitterly disappointed with their new home. The Catholic archbishop of Santa Fe, the Reverend John Baptist Salpointe, stated that the Indians could not live where they had been assigned—the location was on the north side of the White Mountains and would be subject to heavy snows for at least five months each year. It was also located 20 miles from the reservation, and there was not an inch of tillable soil in the area awarded to the Jicarillas.

The Jicarillas adamantly rejected the idea of spending a second winter on the wind-swept mountain, and made their way back to northern New Mexico in small groups during the fall of 1886. The military commanders of the district of New Mexico finally agreed to provide them protection, and Governor Edmund G. Ross of New Mexico consented that they could continue to stay in the northern portion of the territory. The present reservation was finally set aside by executive order of February 11, 1887, and the settlers who had illegally entered and remained on the reservation were finally removed.

5

• • •

CLAIM SUMMARY

The noted anthropologist Frederick Webb Hodge identified the region occupied by the Jicarilla Apaches from the earliest period as that of the mountainous region of southeast Colorado and northern New Mexico and said that their range at various periods extended eastward to western Kansas and Oklahoma and into northwest Texas. He also wrote that the Arkansas, the Rio Grande, and the Canadian rivers figured in the Tribe's genesis myth, and that its traditions seemed centered around Taos and the head of the Arkansas River. This opinion by Mr. Hodge confirmed the use and occupancy of the central area of the claims by the Jicarilla Apaches from time immemorial.

The eminent anthropologist Morris Opler placed the ancient home of the Jicarilla Apaches in a large portion of the central area of the claim bounded on the north by the 37th parallel (the present northern border of New Mexico); on the east by a line running through the town of Springer, New Mexico; on the south by the 36th parallel (a line running through Chimayo, New Mexico); and on the west by Tierra Amarilla.

The writer and anthropologist Oliver La Farge, testifying on deposition in Santa Fe in January 5, 1951, located the ancestral home of the Jicarilla Apaches as the entire central portion of the claim as well as the western portion. Mr. La Farge could correlate his conclusions with early Spanish records and the accountings of the older members of the Tribe. He stated that the ethnological and archaeological evidence fit in perfectly with the Spanish documents; and from all the records he studied, the Jicarillas were occupying the mountains of the central portion of the claim at the same time they were hunting buffalo on the plains as a major occupation.

He further testified that there were no other Indian occupants of the central claim area within historic times; the Utes settled farther north and west, and the Kiowa and Comanches stayed in the flat country.

He described the western portion of the Jicarilla occupancy to be at the boundary of the present reservation, extending from the present reservation southward to Abiquiu. Its eastern boundary ran from the towns of Mora and Wagon Mound in Mora County to the Canadian River; then on a diagonal northward to the intersection of the Oklahoma border and northeastern New Mexico; thence to La Junta, Colorado; thence westerly to Pueblo, Colorado, returning back into the mountains.

He placed the northwestern boundary to the headwaters of the Rio Grande, and testified from his research that Jicarillas were the sole occupants of these areas.

The testimony of older Indians taken at hearings in Santa Fe, and also on deposition, indicated that the Jicarilla Apaches located their places of birth throughout the central area during the eighteenth century and that they resided there, hunting and gathering food throughout the area.

Cevero Caramillo said that his father was born at Cimarron and that his grandparents lived near there. It was their habit to move about the area surrounding Cimarron in their quest for food and dwelling sites; they ranged as far away as Las Vegas, and they hunted buffalo up toward Oklahoma.

Henry L. Vicenti and Juanito Julian also testified that their ancestors had lived along the Cimarron River. Alasco Tisnado was familiar with the areas around Tucumcari and had hunted buffalo "four days travel east of the Canadian River." He said that he was also familiar with many places throughout the central portion of the claim area.

The expert witnesses testifying before the Commission agreed generally that the Jicarilla Apaches occupied and used the central area of the claim from time immemorial until it was taken by the United States. Dr. Alfred B. Thomas testified that the ancestors of the petitioners were found throughout the claim area, including the heartland, from earliest Spanish times through the American period, until the Indians were placed on the reservation in 1887.

Dr. Frank C. Hibben, also testifying for the petitioners, said that based upon the archaeology, ethnology, and anthropology of the area, he had found evidence that the ancestors of the Jicarilla Apaches had lived in the central portion of the claim area back to the earliest times such evidence became available.

Claim Areas

The evidence of Indian title to the extensive claim area was considered in our argument and briefs to the Commission by dividing the claim area into several parts: the central area, the area west of the Rio Grande, and the area north of the Arkansas River.

The Central Area

The evidence on behalf of the Tribe was convincing as to the central portion of the claim area, and the witnesses for the government finally conceded much of this area to the Tribe. The evidence consisted of historical archaeological and ethnological material, reports of American officials, numerous maps, the testimony of older members of the Tribe, and the opinions of various experts.

The history of the claim area shows that the central portion was under Spanish dominion from the sixteenth century until 1821, and that throughout this period Spanish explorers, missionaries, military expeditions, and civilian administrators reported the presence of Jicarilla Apaches in their predecessor bands throughout the central area.

Although the administration of the government of Mexico from 1821 to 1846 provided very few reports of any kind, the few American reports from that period showed the Jicarilla Apaches located in the same central area of the claim.

The evidence concerning Jicarilla Apache occupancy of the area subsequent to 1846 consisted of numerous military reports and communications of Indian agents; continuity of occupation was also substantiated by archaeological evidence. Noted anthropologists identified the region occupied by the Jicarilla Apaches from the early period as that of the mountainous region of southeastern Colorado and northern New Mexico, with their range, at various periods, extending eastward to western Kansas and Oklahoma and into northwestern Texas.

The testimony of the older Indians taken at the hearing in Santa Fe and also on deposition, set forth above, located places of birth of Jicarilla Apaches in the central area during the eighteenth century, where they resided, hunted, and gathered food.

Dr. Alfred B. Thomas testified that the ancestors of the Jicarillas were found throughout the claim area, including the heartland, from earliest Spanish times through the American period, until the Indians were placed upon the reservation by the United States in 1887.

Dr. Hibben, testifying for the Tribe, stated that based on the archaeology, ethnology, and anthropology of the area, he had found evidence that the ancestors of the Tribe had lived throughout the central portion of the claim area from earliest times. The witnesses for the government generally agreed.

Dr. Averam Bender located the Jicarilla Apaches in northeastern New Mexico and northern New Mexico, as far north as the Colorado border (as it existed at the time of the hearing). He agreed that the southern boundary of the claim ran roughly along the 35th parallel (near present-day Interstate 40). His eastern boundary was quite vague, although he conceded that it would run as far east as the Canadian River and that he had no basis for contesting the claim that it extended on to 103° longitude (the Texas border). To the west, Dr. Bender claimed that Jicarilla Apache land use and occupancy extended only to the Sangre de Cristo mountains.

The other government witness, Albert T. Schroeder, described the area of traditional land use and occupancy of the Jicarilla Apaches as extending to the Canadian River on the east; to the Sangre de Cristo Mountains on the west; along a line north of Taos Pueblo on the north; and along a line connecting Pecos, Las Vegas, and Mora on the south. However, the map introduced by the government showed that the bulk of the central area was land used and occupied by the Jicarilla Apaches from time immemorial.

One dispute concerning the claims of the Jicarillas to the central area rose out of the contention originally made by the government that the Ute Indians occupied a portion of the land, but Mr. Schroeder eventually conceded that the Utes were not living in New Mexico prior to the American occupation.

There was also a contention that the eastern boundary of the central area, from the Canadian River to the Texas border, was used and occupied by Comanche and Kiowa Apache Indians, but no evidence was brought forth by counsel for the Comanches (who attended the hearing) to sustain any claim on behalf of these other Indian tribes.

In fact Mr. Schroeder finally conceded that he knew of no valid evidence to support a claim that the Comanches and Kiowa Apaches had ever used or occupied eastern New Mexico.

The archaeological and ethnological evidence supported the conclusion of exclusive use and occupancy of the central area by the Jicarilla Apaches. More than fifty archaeological sites that lay within the central area were positively identified by Dr. Hibben as Jicarilla Apache villages or campsites.

A number of places and landmarks sacred to the Jicarillas were also identified, including the Spanish Peaks, La Veta Butte, Huerfano Butte, Sierra Blanca Mountain (in Colorado), Rabbit Ear Mountain, Sierra Grande, and Tucumcari Butte (in northeastern New Mexico). Dr. Hibben further identified trails used by the Jicarilla Apaches to go between their hunting and gathering grounds.

In the southern and eastern areas of the claim, many permanent and semipermanent village sites were located by Dr.

Hibben, well-provisioned with wood and water and generally on high ground, where the Indians commanded a view of a large expanse of terrain. Dr. Hibben identified over twenty permanent or semipermanent Jicarilla Apache hunting encampments located in eastern New Mexico on the edge of the Piedmont Uplift and on high mesas overlooking the buffalo plains.

In the mountainous portion of the central area of the claim, there were a number of other sites identified by Dr. Hibben. These defensive sites were located on high ground, from which the people could see long distances over an undulating plain where there was good hunting for elk and antelope, as well as buffalo. The Jicarilla Apaches had had permanent villages on these sites, which were positively identified by Juan Dedios.

Although the central portion of the claim covered a large area, the arid and semiarid expanses within the region necessitated constant movement in order to ensure a sufficient food supply. There was no archaeological evidence of settlement by any other people except for the earlier Pueblo Indians within this central area. The Mouache band of Utes hunted with the Jicarilla Apaches for a short period of time, but they were first attracted to the claim area by the establishment of ration points at Abiquiu and Taos in 1853 and thereafter.

The Utes and the Jicarilla Apaches were on friendly terms and traveled and hunted together, but the Utes never regarded the claim area as their territory. In 1868 they were assigned to a reservation north of the 37th parallel and west of 107° longitude, within their ancestral homeland. These western and southern boundaries accepted by the Utes approximate the traditional boundary between the Utes and the Jicarilla Apaches, and coincided with the northwestern border claimed by the Jicarillas. The Ute bands visited temporarily within New Mexico before they moved onto their own lands within a few years after the treaty of 1868.

The evidence on behalf of the Tribe as to the exclusive use and occupancy of the central portion of the plain was uncontroverted by any positive testimony or documentary evidence introduced by the government.

The Area West of the Rio Grande

The claim was made on behalf of the Tribe that the early Jicarilla Apaches exclusively used and occupied areas west of the Rio Grande, extending from the southern border of the claim area to the 37th parallel of latitude (the present northern border of New Mexico) from time immemorial, according to the Jicarilla Indian way of life.

Although the evidence was strong and persuasive as to the occupancy of this area, the Indian Claims Commission found that the Jicarilla Apaches did not use this area exclusively of other tribes prior to the date of American occupancy. The attorneys for the Tribe believe that the Commission was influenced by the extent of the claim area (contrasted with the relatively small population of the Tribe), and that it reduced the award substantially for that reason.

Despite the ruling of the Commission, the evidence, uncontradicted by the government, was strong to the effect that the early Jicarilla Apaches occupied lands west of the Rio Grande. Dr. Thomas so testified, basing his opinion upon the records of Spanish explorations as well as the later history of Indian land use in the nineteenth century.

Dr. Hibben also reached this conclusion, stating that there was a clear boundary along the western edge of the claim area, that there was strong archaeological evidence of occupation by the Jicarilla Apaches within the claim area west of the Rio Grande, and that there existed an abrupt division showing occupation by the Navajos west of that boundary.

As to the specific location of archaeological areas, the Hibben map indicates numerous Jicarilla Apache campsites west of the Rio Grande (map 4). Morris Opler identified the western boundary of Jicarilla Apache country as the line running north and south through Chama, New Mexico, and thus also recognized that portions of the Jicarilla Apache Tribe did occupy and use lands on the west side of the Rio Grande. Oliver La Farge testified that the Jicarillas anciently occupied lands west of the Rio Grande, until they were moved onto the reservation.

The fact that the Jicarilla Apaches were at one time placed on a reservation west of the Rio Grande, and that they were satisfied with this location, also lent support to a conclusion of aboriginal use and occupancy of this area by the Tribe.

Dr. Bender, witness for the government, testified that Jicarilla Apaches were not found west of the Rio Grande prior to 1850, but he based his conclusions solely on the fact that the Indians had requested permission in that year from Governor Calhoun to cross to the west of the river and live there; from this he inferred that they had not previously lived there.

Dr. Bender's conclusion was directly contradicted by evidence in the historical documents that the Jicarilla Apaches were found to the west of the Rio Grande in Spanish times and at the time of the earliest American reports of expeditions. He also testified that the Utes had lived within the claim area west of the Rio Grande in 1850, but this conclusion was rebutted by Governor Meriwether's letter and map of December 30, 1856, both of which show the Utes as being located outside of the claim area, west of the Rio Grande but north of the present Colorado–New Mexico boundary.

The military campaigns by the United States against the Jicarilla Apaches in the early 1850s clearly revealed that the Jicarilla Apaches were familiar with the country west of the Rio Grande; they could not have evaded the military without extensive knowledge of that mountainous terrain. American cavalry pursued the Indians and defeated a force of 150 under Francisco Chacon on the Ojo Caliente River in 1854. Later in the year, it was reported by Agent Messervy that the Jicarilla Apaches were located in the county of Rio Arriba (in northwest New Mexico), west of the Rio Grande. Additional military reports placed the Jicarilla Apaches at Ojo del Gallo, 30 miles south of the San Juan River and west of the Rio Grande, in 1855.

Indian Agent Labadi reported that the Indians were living in the vicinity of the Abiquiu agency later that year. The treaty of 1855 between the Jicarilla Apaches and the United States (never ratified by the U.S. Senate) provided a reservation for the Indians along the Chama River, west of the Rio Grande.

The Indian Claims Commission was clearly wrong in denying the claim of the Jicarilla Apaches to this area.

The Area North of the Arkansas River

Testimony by the older members of the Jicarilla Apache Tribe supported the claim to continued occupation and use of the area north of the Arkansas River. Several of these Indians testified that Pike's Peak was within the land owned by the Jicarilla Apaches. At certain times the Jicarillas lived and hunted in eastern Colorado. Dr. Hibben located sites of Jicarilla villages in this area and found evidence of their occupation and use by the Tribe after the Civil War.

On the western slope of the mountains surrounding the San Luis Valley were sites on Culebra Creek that were common camping places of the Jicarilla Apaches when they moved north to the San Luis Valley to hunt in the mountains for antelope and mountain sheep. This was apparently also the camping place of the "Acho" Apaches mentioned by de Vargas in 1696; it was regularly used through historic times.

Other sites used by the Apaches, as they traveled north to hunt mountain sheep and other game in the Sangre de Cristo mountains of Colorado, were on Indian Creek (north of Fort Garland), and at Redwing (north of the Huerfano River). The archaeological evidence of occupancy on these sites included pottery (both Jicarilla and Spanish), manos, scrapers, broad-bladed arrowheads (some of iron), brass dangles, tipi rings, and camp debris.

These sites were mentioned by the informant Juan Dedios as camping places of the Jicarilla Apaches, when they traveled from New Mexico into Colorado to hunt mountain sheep, and when they moved into the Huerfano Valley. The presence of Spanish ware as well as modern tools indicated the use of these sites from the Spanish period through American times.

The Indian Claims Commission, in denying the Jicarilla Apaches the area north of the Arkansas River, apparently relied partly on the Treaty of Fort Laramie, in which the southern boundary of the Cheyenne and Arapahoe claim was defined as the line running from the headwaters of the Arkansas River "thence down the Arkansas River to the crossing of the Santa Fe Road." However, in 1860–61, Commissioner A. B. Greenwood, assisted by other government agents, attempted to establish the Cheyenne and Arapahoe tribes on a reservation along the Arkansas River, later the area of the Jicarilla Apache claim. An agency was established for these tribes at Fort Wise (later Fort Lyon), and strenuous efforts were made to induce them to settle on this reservation. These efforts failed, however, and none of the Cheyenne or Arapahoe bands could be induced to remain permanently within the area. These tribes were finally convened at a treaty council held in 1865, in which the Colorado reservation was abolished and a new reservation was assigned them, outside the Jicarilla Apache claim area.

The Commission's denial of the the Jicarilla Apache's claim to lands north of the Arkansas led the attorneys to conclude that the Commission desired to cut down the extent of the claim because it evidently believed the claim encompassed more area than the Tribe required for its hunting-and-gathering way of life. Besides being extremely discouraging for the Tribe, the Commission's findings were simply historically indefensible.

6

• • •

COMMISSION FINDINGS

The Indian Claims Commission issued its interlocutory order and findings of fact on the boundaries of the Jicarilla Apache claim on August 26, 1963. This order, 12 I.C.C. 439 (1963) (not compiled) read as follows:

> Upon the findings of fact and opinion this day filed herein, and which are hereby made a part of this order, the Commission finds and concludes as a matter of law:
>
> 1. That, the petitioner, the Jicarilla Apache Tribe of the Jicarilla Apache Reservation, is an organized tribe of American Indians, and, as such, has the right to bring and maintain the claims in Docket 22-A in a representative capacity for and on behalf of the aboriginal Jicarilla Apache Tribe pursuant to the provisions of the Indian Claims Commission Act (60 Stat. 1049, Chap. 959);
>
> 2. That, by virtue of the Treaty of Guadalupe Hidalgo, entered into between the United States and the Mexican Republic on February 2, 1848 (9 Stat. 922), the United States acquired by formal cession control and sovereignty over a vast area south of Arkansas River embracing a great part of the aboriginal claim of the Jicarilla Apache Tribe herein;
>
> 3. That, during the years following the attachment of American sovereignty in 1848 until the Jicarilla Apache Tribe was finally settled on the reservation in Rio Arriba County, New Mexico, the United States, without payment of compensation and through the actions and conduct of its military forces, other agents and the white citizenry, gradually acquired

> the aboriginal lands of the Jicarilla Apache Tribe as more particularly described in the Commission's Finding 60;
>
> IT IS THEREFORE ORDERED that this case shall proceed for the determination of the acreage of that area as set forth in the Commission's Finding 60, all relevant matters concerning Spanish and Mexican land grants within said area, and for purposes of the evaluation, the time or times said area was acquired by the United States, provided, however, that, if the parties should mutually agree on said date or dates of evaluation of the lands awarded herein, subject to the approval of the Commission, then this case shall proceed with the hearing on valuation.

Finding of Fact 60, 12 I.C.C. 439, 467 (1963), referred to in the order, was as follows:

> **Finding 60.** The Commission finds that (except for the lands in the Spanish and Mexican land grants to be determined in the next phase of these proceedings—see Finding No. 59 ante) there was an area largely in northeast New Mexico, with a small area in southeast Colorado to which the Jicarilla Apache Tribe held original Indian title, which area is described as follows:
>
> Commencing with the present location of the town of McIntosh, New Mexico; thence north along the course of the Atchison, Topeka and Santa Fe railroad line as shown on the map of New Mexico (Pet. Ex. B-21) to the present site of Glorieta, N.M., shown on the same map; thence north to the crest of Santa Fe Baldy Mountain; thence northeasterly along the crest of the Sangre de Cristo range of mountains to the south bank of the Rio Chiquito river; thence east along the south bank of said river to the town Black Lake, N.M.; thence north to the most easterly point of Eagle Nest Lake, in New Mexico; thence clockwise along said lake to its most northerly point; thence westward in a straight line to the mouth of the Rio Hondo; thence in a northeasterly direction along the west bank of the Rio Grande river to its point of intersection with the present southern boundary of

> the State of Colorado; thence northeast to the present townsite of Trinidad, Colorado; thence southeast to the northeast corner of the State of New Mexico; thence south along the east boundary of the State of New Mexico to its intersection with 35°30' of north latitude; thence west along 35°30' of north latitude to the intersection of 103°30' west longitude; thence south along 103°30' west longitude to its intersection with 34°50' of north latitude; thence west along 34°50' north latitude to the point of beginning.

Maps of the claim area and award area are described in Finding 60 (see maps 4 and 6).

The Commission issued an opinion on the same date, August 26, 1963, which set forth the history of the claim and discussed certain legal matters, including objections made by the government concerning stipulations between attorneys for the Jicarilla Apaches and the Pueblo Indians as to their respective boundaries, as well as questions of jurisdiction.

The Commission denied those objections and also disposed of a claim by the government that the sovereignty and occupancy of the Spanish prevented any occupancy by the Jicarilla Apache Tribe as now constituted and that this prior Spanish possession prevented the Jicarillas from acquiring any occupancy rights to the claim lands. The Commission held that the evidence did not support the government's contention and that the Spaniards did not dispossess the Jicarillas.

Subsequent Proceedings

The attorneys proceeded to work on the date of taking of tribal lands by the United States and on the questions of compensation for Spanish and Mexican land grants. Soon after the order of the Commission was entered, other experts were hired.

First a determination was made of the total acreage of the lands awarded and the acreage of Spanish and Mexican land grants included within the award area. The government and the tribal attorneys were in agreement that the acreage within

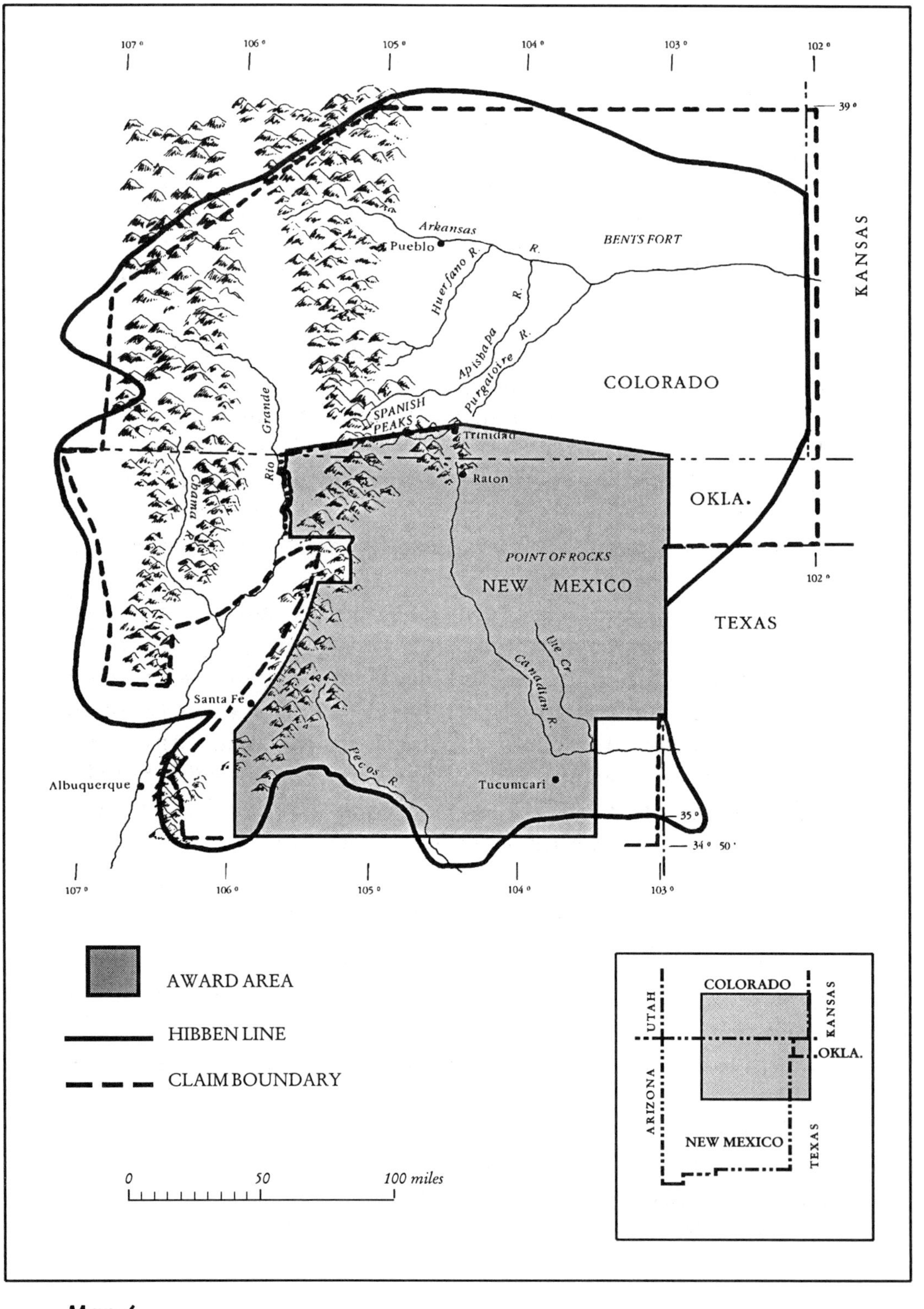

Map 6
Jicarilla Apache Award Area

the boundaries described in the Commission's Finding 60, including confirmed land grants, was 14,026,000 acres, and that the area of the twenty-two confirmed Spanish and Mexican land grants within the area was 4,807,467.23 acres. The total land-grant acreage was deducted from the total acreage of the claim, leaving a net acreage of 9,218,532.77 acres.

The attorneys proceeded to gather evidence as to the date of taking, as well as information on the land grants. The government contended that the land-grant lands were taken by the Spanish and Mexican governments, not by the United States, and therefore the United States should not be liable for compensation for these lands. The attorneys for the Tribe, however, contended that the Indians had continued to use and occupy the land-grant lands, except for those small areas occupied by land-grant towns and by ranches within the land-grant areas; therefore the land-grant lands had not actually been taken by Spain or Mexico. The government also claimed that the lands were taken from the Tribe in the early 1850s, when Kearney occupied New Mexico. The attorneys for the Tribe contended, in contrast, that the lands were not actually taken from the Indians until they were deprived of their use and occupancy; they had in fact continued to hunt and gather freely on their ancestral lands until they were placed on a reservation.

These were the issues to be tried in the second phase of the proceeding.

PART II

• • •

THE SECOND PHASE

7

• • •

LIABILITY FOR LAND GRANTS

In the first phase, the Indian Claims Commission determined that the Jicarilla Apache Tribe had Indian title to certain lands in northeastern New Mexico and southeastern Colorado; that the United States was liable for the taking of these lands without the consent of the Tribe; and that the United States had not made payments of compensation for the acquired land. The Commission also determined the exterior boundaries of the taken lands, here referred to as the "award area."

In the second phase, the issues for determination were the liability of the United States for the taking of certain Spanish and Mexican land-grant lands located within the award area, and the date of valuation and the acreage of the lands for whose taking the United States was liable.

As mentioned above, after the first decision by the Commission determining the extent of the claimed lands, the government and tribal attorneys agreed that the acreage within the boundaries described in the Commission's Finding 60, including confirmed land grants, was 14,026,000 acres, and that the area of the twenty-two confirmed Spanish and Mexican land grants within the area was 4,807,467.23 acres. The total land-grant acreage was deducted from the total acreage of the claim, leaving the acreage to be valued at 9,218,532.77 acres.

From December 7 through December 16,1964, the Commission received the testimony and exhibits of the government and the Tribe on the issues for determination. The Tribe contended that the Spanish and Mexican governments made land grants to non-Indians within the award area subject to Jicarilla Apache title and that this Jicarilla title was taken from the Tribe by the United States without payment of compensation.

The Tribe contended that the Spanish and Mexican governments retained all minerals in land-grant lands and that their rights continued as public property. The Tribe also contended that certain portions of these land-grant lands, as they were surveyed by the United States surveyor general, were, in fact, public domain subject to Jicarilla Indian title when the award area was under Spanish and Mexican sovereignty and that the Jicarilla title to those lands was taken by the United States without payment of compensation.

There was no treaty between the United States and the Tribe constituting a legal taking of the land.

The Tribe further claimed that Jicarilla title to the award area, including land-grant lands, was taken by the United States in 1883, the year when the Tribe's use and occupancy of the award area was effectively eliminated, and when the Tribe was deprived of, and removed from, the award-area lands.

The government contended that the land-grant lands were to be removed from the acreage for which the United States was liable, once it had been shown that there was a grant confirmed by the United States Congress and the acreage of the grant had been established by survey. The government contended that the date of taking was either 1853 or 1860, without any evidence to support these dates.

The Expert Witnesses

The Tribe's expert witnesses were Dr. Frank C. Hibben, professor of anthropology at the University of New Mexico; Dr. Leroy Gordon, professor of geography at the University of New Mexico; Dr. Donald C. Cutter, professor of history at the University of New Mexico; and Dr. John Maktos, a distinguished lawyer and specialist in international affairs.

Dr. Gordon graduated from San Francisco State College and received his Ph.D. at the University of California at Berkeley. His publications included a study of the northwestern part of Colombia, *Human Geography and Ecology in the Sinu Country of Colombia,* and a study of the Terib Indians of western Panama.

In connection with the Jicarilla Apache land claim, the Department of Geography at the University of New Mexico entered into a research contract with the Tribe to study the settlement and land use of the Jicarilla Apache area. A report was prepared in 1960, with reference to the original claimed area, and was then revised to refer to the smaller award area.

Dr. Hibben's qualifications were presented to the Commission at the original hearing; in addition to the work he had done in preparation for the 1958 hearing, he had reviewed his previous research in 1964, in preparation for the December, 1964 hearing, including revisits to numerous sites and additional excavations. His 1964 work focused on evidence of use of the various Jicarilla sites in the award area after 1865.

Dr. Cutter was a professor of southwestern history at the University of New Mexico. He received his bachelor's degree in Spanish and his master's and doctorate degrees in history (with a minor in anthropology) at the University of California at Berkeley. In 1947 and 1948, Dr. Cutter was a Fellow in Pacific Coast History of the Native Sons of the Golden West at the University of California. In 1949 and 1950 he had done research in Spain and Mexico, under a Social Science Research Council Research Training Fellowship. In 1953 he held the Del Amo Foundation Fellowship in Spain. In 1961 and 1962 he was a Fulbright Research Fellow in Spain. He taught at San Diego State College in California for one year, at the University of Southern California from 1951 to 1956, and became professor of southwestern history at the University of New Mexico in 1962. Dr. Cutter authored a number of publications involving Indian exploration and had done research on the history of Spanish and Mexican land grants in California. His studies included land-grant history in connection with this case, relying on microfilms of New Mexico land grants.

Dr. Maktos had studied at Oxford, Harvard, and the University of Paris. His field of doctoral study was comparative and international law. He practiced law in Paris for a short period and completed his advanced degree at Harvard in conflicts of law, international law, jurisprudence, and Roman law. After securing his doctorate degree, he entered the Legal Advisor's Office of the U.S. State Department in 1929 and remained there, in the field of private international law, until his retirement in 1962. He was chief counsel of the American-Mexican Claims Commission in 1944 and 1945 and chief of the division of the United Nations Latin American Affairs Division from 1945 to 1953. In his State Department work, he dealt with the law of discovery and the law of property rights of local and native populations in connection with discovery and change of sovereignty. He had made extensive study of the land laws of Mexico and the relation of the laws of Spain and Mexico to property rights, including the property rights of native people.

The government's expert witnesses were Dr. Howard C. F. Cline, head of the Hispanic Foundation of the Library of Congress, who had studied Indian village life in southern Mexico and, for the purposes of this case, had compiled statistical data on Spanish and Mexican land grants in New Mexico; and Dr. Harold H. Dunham, professor of history at the University of Denver, who had made a study of land occupation and use in New Mexico, mainly by New Mexican and Pueblo Indian populations around the year 1848.

Testimony and Exhibits

The Tribe's evidence at the hearing was based on studies made by Dr. Gordon, including a study entitled "Environment, Settlement and Land Use in the Jicarilla Apache Claim Area." Also included was a map prepared by Dr. Gordon, showing the dates of survey plats and field notes of nearly all the townships in the award area (except for the land-grant areas), made by the United States surveyor general; it indicated wire fences present at the time of survey and showed the general extent of settlement and categories of land use at that time (see map 7). Also admitted into evidence were survey plats and notes of Spanish

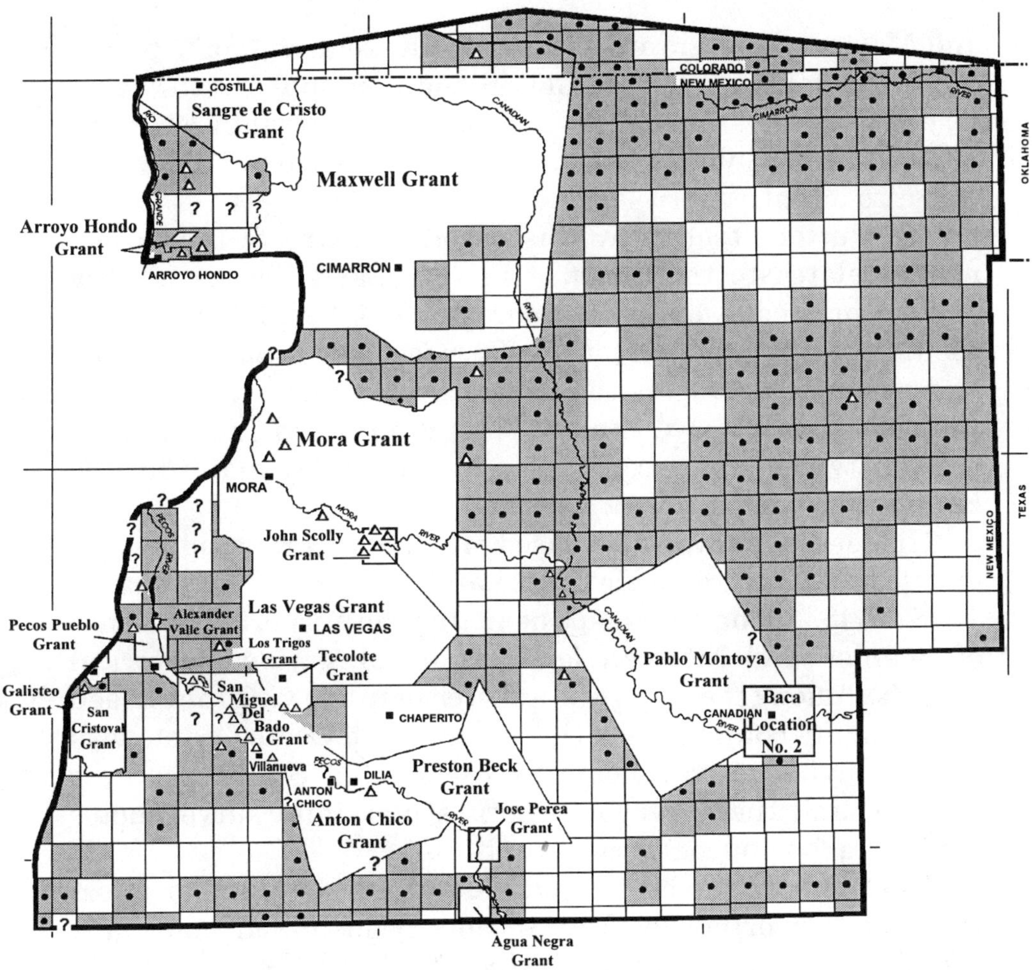

JICARILLA APACHE TRIBE
V.
UNITED STATES
DOCKET NO. 22-A
EXHIBIT NO. PLG-4

- [ ] Townships for which there is no evidence of use, improvements, or occupancy.
- [shaded] Townships used for grazing purposes only.
- [•] Townships upon which cattle ranches were located and which are noted as being, or presumed to have been, used for grazing.
- [△] Settlements.
- [?] Townships for which we have no notes nor plats.

Map 7
Dr. Gordon's Map of New Mexico Townships and Land Grants in the Award Area

and Mexican land grants within the award area, made by the Surveyor General's Office, and, in addition, maps of the territory of New Mexico made by the surveyor general in 1876 and 1879. A map of public surveys in Colorado territory dated 1866 was also admitted.

Dr. Cutter's testimony was based on extracts from documents related to the Court of Private Land Claims in New Mexico, printed by order of Congress, 1854–89, and portions of the *Recopilación de Leyes de los Reynos de las Indias.* He cited *Federal Indian Law,* by the United States Department of the Interior, and his own study, "An Inquiry into Indian Land Rights," which was accompanied by an overlay map showing land grants within the award area.

His testimony was also based on a report prepared by him entitled "Spanish and Mexican Land Grants in New Mexico, 1698–1848," along with maps depicting the purported presence of Spanish and Mexican land grants at various historical periods. Among the maps was a sketch map showing the alleged approximate boundaries of the unconfirmed Ocate Grant, with accompanying survey notes by the United States surveyor general, and the surveyor general's plats and survey notes regarding four unconfirmed grants.

Dr. Dunham's exhibits consisted of a large number of extracts, taken primarily from secondary historical materials; *The Seventh Census of the United States, 1850*; *The Census of the United States, 1870*; various exhibits pertaining to opinions of the Court of Private Land Claims; and a map of certain trails within the award area.

The testimony of the government and the Tribe was also based on two joint exhibits introduced at the hearings. One, a map of the award area prepared by the Bureau of Land Management, showed the Spanish and Mexican land grants in the award area as they were surveyed and patented by the U.S. surveyor general and listed the total acreage of the award area, along with acreage measurements of the surveyed grants. Also introduced was a tabulation prepared by Dr. Gordon of the number of township surveys made within the award area in

Chart 1

Land Grants, by Size

Grants	Award Area (acres)
Sangre de Cristo	279,700
Maxwell	1,642,000
Arroyo Hondo	18,900
Antoine Leroux	16,500
Valle	1,242
Pueblo de Pecos	18,763
Los Trigos	9,647
San Miguel del Bado	5,148
San Cristoval	81,033
Galisteo	261
Agua Negra	17,361
Lamy	8,400
Pablo Montoya & Baca Location No. 2	708,800
Mora, Las Vegas, Tecolote, & Scolly	1,303,300
Antonio Ortiz	163,921
Preston Beck, Anton Chico & Perea	584,600
TOTAL ACRES	4,859,576

SOURCE: Exh. PLG, p. 5-26, 28, and 29

each year by the United States surveyor general from 1856 through 1900.

Acreage Stipulations

The stipulations regarding the land grants and the acreage within the award area are summarized in chart 1.

The parties also stipulated that the Baca Location no. 2 was not a valid grant by Spain or Mexico prior to the cession of the award area to the United States in 1848 and that the portion of the grant that did not overlap with the Pablo Montoya Grant was to be included within the lands taken by the United States, for which the Tribe was to receive payment of compensation. They also agreed that the acreage not overlapping the surveyed Pablo Montoya Grant was 52,109 acres.

Spanish and Mexican Land Grants

New Mexico, Texas, Arizona, and California were subject to four categories of land distribution under the laws of Spain and, later, Mexico. Two of them, the Pueblo Indian aboriginal rights and the *empresario* system, were not relevant to the land claim, but the *rancho* (private grants) and the *pueblo* ("town" or community grants) systems were widely used throughout the Southwest and were thus pertinent to the case (see chart 2).

Private grants were given to one or two persons and contained no provision for the subsequent distribution of the granted land. Town grants were given to large groups of individuals, but they also contained no provision for a subsequent distribution of land within the area.

Based on his study of international law, the Tribe's legal expert, Dr. Maktos, testified that there existed a legal principle adopted by all European nations dealing with the New World that regulated the acquisition of land, including areas now constituting the United States. This principle held that the title obtained by the European discovering nations was subject to native rights of use and occupancy of the land. Dr. Maktos testified that Spain had accepted this principle and that the recognition of Indian use and occupancy by Spain included the rights of settlement upon lands under cultivation and the rights of hunting game, fishing, and searching for berries and other plant life for sustenance. The right of use applied not only to agricultural tribes but to hunting tribes as well.

Recognized use and occupancy, which was honored by Spain, referred to occupancy belonging to a certain tribe, to the exclusion of other tribes. This was the so-called aboriginal title.

Chart 2

Confirmed Spanish and Mexican Land Grants

Type and Name of Grant	Date of Grant
Spanish Private Grants	
Antoine Leroux	1742
Los Trigos	1813
Alexander Valle	1815
Antonio Ortiz	1819
John Lamy	1820
Spanish Town Grants	
Pueblo de Pecos	1659
San Miguel del Bado	1794
Arroyo Hondo	1815
Mexican Private Grants	
Preston Beck	1823
Agua Negra	1824
Pablo Montoya	1824
Perea	1825
San Cristoval	1827
Maxwell	1841
Sangre de Cristo	1843
Scolly	1845
Mexican Town Grants	
Las Vegas	1821
Anton Chico	1822
Galisteo	1822
Tecolote	1824
Mora	1835

SOURCE: Exh. PLG, 5-26, 28, and 29

Aboriginal rights can be permanently abandoned by the Indian tribe occupying particular land under international law. However, if the Indians were *forced* to abandon their lands, that abandonment could not be considered a legal abandonment, nor would abandonment exist if the tribe merely, for seasonal periods, migrated to another piece of land and returned to its permanent habitat later.

Dr. Maktos testified that there was no basis in international law for distinguishing between savage or "outlaw" Indians and Indians who lived in settled communities or pueblos. The only distinction was whether there was exclusive occupancy and use.

The Jicarilla Apaches were friends and allies of the Spaniards and Mexicans from earliest times until the United States occupation. Governor Juan Flores de Sierra y Valdez stated in 1754 that it was extremely important to the security of the province (of New Mexico) to conserve the Jicarillas' friendship and to hold it without force. Governor Cachupín made a similar report in 1754. Governor Anza used the Jicarillas as guides and allies in defeating the Comanches in 1779; considered valued allies, the Jicarillas' rights to the use and occupancy of their lands were necessarily respected all the more. The assertions of the government experts, Dr. Dunham and Dr. Cline, with reference to "savage tribes" had no application to the Jicarilla Apaches.

Dr. Maktos knew of no instance in which the government of Spain entered into an agreement to buy Indian land rights, although he admitted that it was possible.

The principle of recognition of Indian property rights under Spanish law continued after the Mexican Revolution of 1821, because Mexico was the successor state to Spain and inherited the law of Spain. Under international law, upon succession of states, the succeeding states must recognize acquired property rights. Mexico not only succeeded in the recognition of native property rights, but the status of the native Indians in the territory to which it succeeded was enhanced by the Plan of Iguala, which provided that all people residing within the Mexican Republic, regardless of race or nationality, were citizens of Mexico with the enjoyment of all civil rights.

Dr. Maktos also testified that unless the granting papers

expressly abolished Indian rights of occupancy, the grants were subject to those Indian rights. It was, therefore, necessary for anyone claiming title free of the Indian right of use and occupancy to prove that that right had been extinguished.

Thus the Indian Claims Commission would be forced to examine the granting language of each grant to determine if it was silent with regard to Indian aboriginal rights; if there was affirmative language indicating that a tort had been committed by the prior sovereign; or if affirmative language existed showing that the granting sovereign intended that the grant respect Indian property rights.

Since Spanish and Mexican law recognized the Indians' right of use and occupancy, and since land grants made by Spain or Mexico were subject to these rights, land grants to non-Indians by the Spanish and Mexican governments were grants subject to the rights of Indians and merely gave the grantees the right to deal with the Indians if they aspired to extinguish Indian rights of use and occupancy. These grants were therefore not a taking by Spain or Mexico.

When the government of the United States took possession of New Mexico, it inherited the obligation to recognize and enforce these Indian rights. When the United States gave patents to the Mexican and Spanish grantees or their successors by act of Congress or through the Court of Private Land Claims, these were quitclaims of its rights to the granted lands. Indian rights of use and occupancy continued, because the patents did not extinguish these rights. Thus the United States took these lands from the Jicarilla Apaches only when it forced them off the grant lands, not before.

The Legal Background

The European nations acquired sovereignty over newly discovered lands, including North America, by a symbolic act whereby representatives of the European sovereign took possession and claimed exclusive jurisdiction over the discovered lands for their sovereign.

The approximate date of occupation by Spain of present-day New Mexico was 1603. Santa Fe was founded in 1611. Except for the interruption caused by the Pueblo Revolt of 1680, Spanish occupation continued until the Mexican Revolution of 1820.

The Council of the Indies was created in Spain in 1511 for the administration of Spain's New World colonies. The objectives of the council with respect to the Indians were to make them, as rapidly as possible, subjects of Spain, taxpayers, and Christians.

In the sixteenth century, there were contemporary statements as to the rights of the Indians in the conquered lands. Particularly significant was that of the Jesuit theologican Francisco de Vitoria, who was asked by Charles V to comment upon the rights of aborigines in the conquered area. In 1532 he stated, "Since the Indians were the true owners of the lands, discovery could not be a basis for conveyance of title—for discovery can be justified only where property is ownerless; nor could title be claimed upon divine rights of the Emperor or the Pope, or in the absence of a just war, only voluntary consent of the aborigines would justify annexation of this territory." The Spanish accepted this doctrine of de Vitoria, which was applied to all Indians, not just to the sedentary tribes.

The *Recopilación de Leyes de los Reynos de las Indias* was an official codification of Spanish law that brought together all decrees that had previously been passed with regard to the Indies. It was generally applied throughout the Indies, including New Mexico.

The *Recopilación* contained laws for the protection of the Indians. For example the discoverers were enjoined from engaging in wars with the Indians or doing them any damage or taking their trade or property. It ordered that distribution of lands be carried out without harm to the Indians, that lands not be given out in prejudice to the Indians and that lands already given out be returned to their owners, and required that Indians be allowed to possess land.

The Spanish Administration

The Spanish authorities in the New World and North America generally adhered to the policies set forth in the *Recopilación*. Local authorities were not permitted to grant land that was in the possession of the Indians to individuals. The history of Spanish administration on the northern frontier, particularly in New Mexico, clearly showed that the protection of Indian lands set forth in the *Recopilación* extended to all Indians, whether they were hunting tribes or sedentary. The policies were particulary applicable to Indians considered to be friendly. The Spanish authorities did not interfere with the use of aboriginal lands by the hunting tribes, nor did they grant land to non-Indians except for locations specifically designated as places for non-Indian settlement.

This was the policy that was adhered to with the Jicarilla Apaches, who maintained friendly relations with the Spaniards. The Jicarillas and the Spanish fought together against the Comanches, and the Spanish used Jicarilla Apache warriors for auxiliary troops in campaigns against the Comanche invasion of their territory.

The Mexican Period

The pattern of respect for Indian rights continued after Mexican independence, until occupation by the United States. Upon the independence of Mexico in 1821, the revolutionary pronouncement of Agustín Iturbide of February 24, 1821, known as the Plan of Iguala, became a fixed principle of Mexican law. Under that plan, the Indians, who had done much to assure victory in the revolution against Spain, became citizens of Mexico, with the right to be employed in any post according to their merits and virtues; their rights and their property rights, in particular, were to be respected and protected by the government. These provisions applied to all Indians in New Mexico.

The Treaty of Guadalupe Hidalgo

In 1848, at the conclusion of the Mexican War with the United States, the Treaty of Guadalupe Hidalgo was signed. Under this treaty the United States agreed to recognize all property rights of former Mexican citizens. Article 8 of the treaty provided that the inhabitants of New Mexico would be free to continue to live in New Mexico or to move to the Mexican Republic, with rights to retain their property or dispose of it as they saw fit. Those who preferred to remain in the territories could retain the title and rights of Mexican citizens or acquire those of citizens of the United States. They were required to make an election within one year if they desired to become U.S. citizens (articles 8 and 9 are set out above, pp. 5–6). The last paragraph of article 8 (9 Stat. 922), provided:

> In the said territories, property of every kind, now belonging to Mexicans not established there, shall be inviolably respected. The present owners, the heirs of these, and all Mexicans who may hereafter acquire said property by contract, shall enjoy with respect to it guaranties equally ample as if the same belonged to citizens of the United States.

Article 9 of the treaty provided that Mexicans in the territory who decided to remain would be admitted at the proper time to the enjoyment of all the rights of citizens of the United States, be protected in the free enjoyment of their liberty and property, and be secured in the free exercise of their religion without restriction.

Although Indians had equal rights as citizens under the Mexican Plan of Iguala, the United States failed to observe the provisions of the Treaty of Guadalupe Hidalgo with respect to Indians, who were not granted full rights of citizenship until June 24, 1924 (Indian Citizenship Act of 1924, 43 Stat. 253, Chap. 233).

Confirmation of Spanish and Mexican Land Grants

An act of Congress of July 22, 1854, directed the surveyor general of New Mexico to review and prepare reports on the nature and validity of all Spanish land grants made by Spanish or Mexican governments in lands within the territory of New Mexico.

The U.S. surveyor general reported his findings on the land-grant claims to Congress at various times after 1854. These reports include the original granting papers, if any, and other evidence found by the surveyor general that indicated the nature of the grants, including information on use and occupancy of the granted areas (see chart 3).

Chart 3

Confirmed Town Grants within Award Area

Name of Grant	Surveyed Acreage
Mora	818,621
Las Vegas	431,653
Anton Chico	378,537
Tecolote	48,123
Arroyo Hondo	18,900
Pueblo de Pecos	18,763
San Miguel del Bado	5,148
Galisteo	261
TOTAL ACRES	1,720,006

SOURCE: Exh. PLG, 5-26, 28, and 29

In general the sizes of the various grants were described in the original granting papers in terms of natural or artificial boundaries that were often vague and subject to disintegration or removal. The surveyor general's reports to Congress did not place an acreage measurement on the size of the grants, but rather reported the surveyor general's decisions as to the validity of the grants only in terms of the descriptive boundaries.

The surveyor general made his investigations and reported his decisions to Congress on claims to all but three of the confirmed Spanish and Mexican land grants within the award area. The claims to the three remaining grants were settled by the Court of Private Land Claims, established in 1891; they were the Galisteo Grant (confirmed in 1899) and the Arroyo Hondo and San Miguel del Bado grants (both confirmed in 1901).

The act of June 21, 1860, confirmed fourteen land grants in the award area. These were the Preston Beck, Sangre de Cristo, Los Trigos, Scolly, Lamy, Agua Negra, Beaubien-Miranda-Maxwell, Perea, Valle, San Cristoval, Las Vegas, Anton Chico, Mora, and Baca locations. The act of December 22, 1858, confirmed the Pueblo de Pecos and Tecolote grants, and the act of March 3, 1869, confirmed the Pablo Montoya, Antonio Ortiz, and Antoine Leroux grants (map 7).

As stated expressly in the acts of 1858, 1860, and 1869, the effect of these confirmation acts was only to give a quitclaim on the part of the United States of any claims it had to the lands determined to have been granted to persons by the Spanish or Mexican governments; but the confirmation was not to affect the adverse rights of any other person or persons whatsoever. These acts ordered the surveyor general of New Mexico to proceed to make the surveys and establish the locations of the grants according to the descriptions set forth in the granting papers.

Except for one grant, the acts did not indicate the acreage measurements to be attributed to the confirmed grants in the award area. The confirmations were made solely in reference to the surveyor general's reports, which included only the boundary descriptions of the original granting papers. However, the Senate Committee on Private Land Claims, when it reported the act of June 21, 1860, to the Senate, declared that it would be guided by the Mexican Colonization Law of 1824—which allowed each grantee eleven square leagues of land.

Under Spanish law and practice, a four-league area was established surrounding each grant. This four-league limit was to be distributed in individual ownership for housing or private fields. The portions of the grants not allotted to individuals, including areas outside the four leagues consisting of pasture and woodlands, formed common lands around the town available for use by any person.

Although town authorities controlled the common lands to some extent, the Spanish crown retained final control and disposition of such lands; after Mexican independence, the Mexican government succeeded and retained control of these lands.

The grant to the town of Las Vegas was similar to other such grants, and the history of that grant confirms the position taken by attorneys for the Tribe that the common lands were free to all and that the Indians were not deprived of the use and occupancy of those lands by the Spanish or Mexican governments.

The U.S. surveyor general's proceedings for confirmation of the Las Vegas Grant indicate that the grant was awarded to twenty-five persons in 1825, as a town grant. The proceedings record the distribution of land to individual villagers within the grant area by name and amount, totalling 27,087 *varas* of land (slightly under 5.5 leagues), or approximately 24,200 acres. Part of the granting document provided that:

> The land contained within the boundaries expressed in this petition is granted not only to the petitioners and the residents of El Bado, but also in general to all who may be destitute of lands to cultivate, provided that the grant to these lands is made on condition that the pasture and watering places are free to all.

Only 24,200 acres of the Las Vegas Grant were allotted to settlers; 407,453 acres were common land, according to Mexican custom and law. The public-land character of these common lands in the Las Vegas Grant still exists under the present laws of the State of New Mexico (secs. 4-6-1 to 4-6-14, NMSA 1978).

Similar language was contained in the Anton Chico Grant, the Tecolote Grant, the Arroyo Hondo Grant, and other town grants. The respect to be accorded to third parties, including Indians, was explicit in the granting papers of the Arroyo Hondo Grant:

> . . . which tract I consider, upon evidence and experience, does not injure either the Indians, it being outside of their league, or the neighbors, the water and pasturage remaining common for the general benefit.

The acreage of common lands in the Mora, Las Vegas, Anton Chico, Tecolote, Arroyo Hondo, Pueblo de Pecos, and San Miguel del Bado grants totaled 1,658,765 acres. The acreage of town allotments within those grants was only 44,181 acres. It was the contention of the Tribe that there was no deprivation of use and occupancy of the common lands. In other words only 44,181 acres of the total acreage of the town grants should have been deducted from the acreage awarded to the Tribe.

Although the Spanish did not adopt colonization laws applicable to New Mexico, the independent Mexican regime, after 1821, issued the Colonization Laws of 1824 and 1828, which pertained to the distribution of land throughout the Mexican empire. These laws are set forth in *Spanish and Mexican Land Laws: New Spain and Mexico* (Mathew G. Reynolds). Section 12 of the Colonization Law of 1824 provided that:

> It shall not be allowed that more than one square league of more than one hundred thousand *varas* [error in original; a square league of land contains 25 million *varas*] of irrigable land, four of temporal land, and six of rangelands, be united as the property of a single hand [thus, under the Law of 1824, the limit per grantee was 11 square leagues of land].

The Colonization Law of 1828 provided that governors of the territories be authorized to grant vacant lands to the families of private persons who made request for such lands for the purpose of habitation or cultivation. The law set forth the conditions under which grants were to be made.

According to Dr. Maktos, the tribes' private grants were to be limited to 11 square leagues of land (approximately 48,400 acres). It is clear that the Maxwell, Pablo Montoya, Preston Beck, Sangre de Cristo, and Antonio Ortiz grants greatly exceeded the maximum allowed under Mexican law; the surveyor general simply ignored the legal limitations (see chart 4).

Chart 4

Confirmed Private Grants within the Award Area

Name of Grant	Surveyed Acreage
Maxwell	1,642,000
Pablo Montoya	655,000
Preston Beck	318,699
Sangre de Cristo	279,700
Arroyo Hondo	18,900
Antonio Ortiz	163,922
San Cristoval	81,033
Scolly	21,701
Perea	17,712
Agua Negra	17,361
Antoine Leroux	16,500
Los Trigos	9,647
Lamy	8,400
Valle	1,242
TOTAL ACRES	3,232,917

SOURCE: Exh. PLG, 5-26, 28, and 29

The history of the Maxwell Grant is illustrative (map 8). The grant was originally made in 1841 to Charles Beaubien and Guadalupe Miranda, one of whom said, when a protest was raised against the grant, "The grant does not exceed 15 to 18 leagues." The grant described the boundaries in terms of rivers and mountains, without any other survey descriptions.

The 1877 survey plat showed that the acreage of the grant within the award area was approximately 1,640,000 acres. The survey included the towns of Rayado, Elizabethtown, Vermejo, Clifton, and Cimarron, and gave the population of Cimarron as eight hundred persons.

The grant expressly stated that it was issued for the purpose of improving the acreage without imparting injury to any third party. The Pablo Montoya, Preston Beck, Sangre de Cristo, and other private land grants all contained similar language. It was clear that these private grants, like the town grants, were issued on the condition that the grantees cultivate the land and that grazing lands remain common lands available to all. Dr. Maktos testified that this was true, even though the granting papers did not explicitly state that the pastures and water were common to all.

Land Grants and the Tribe

As set forth above, an important issue in the 1964 hearings was the liability of the United States to the Jicarilla Apache Tribe for land-grant lands within the claim area; the attorneys for the Tribe contended that they were taken by the United States, while the government contended that they were taken from the Tribe by Spanish and Mexican governments, which deprived the members of the Tribe of use and occupancy of the land during their occupations.

The issue was ultimately decided against the Tribe. The attorneys now believe that the Commission considered that the Tribe (with its limited population at the time of the award) was not entitled to more than the nine million acres awarded and that to allow compensation for land-grant lands would have

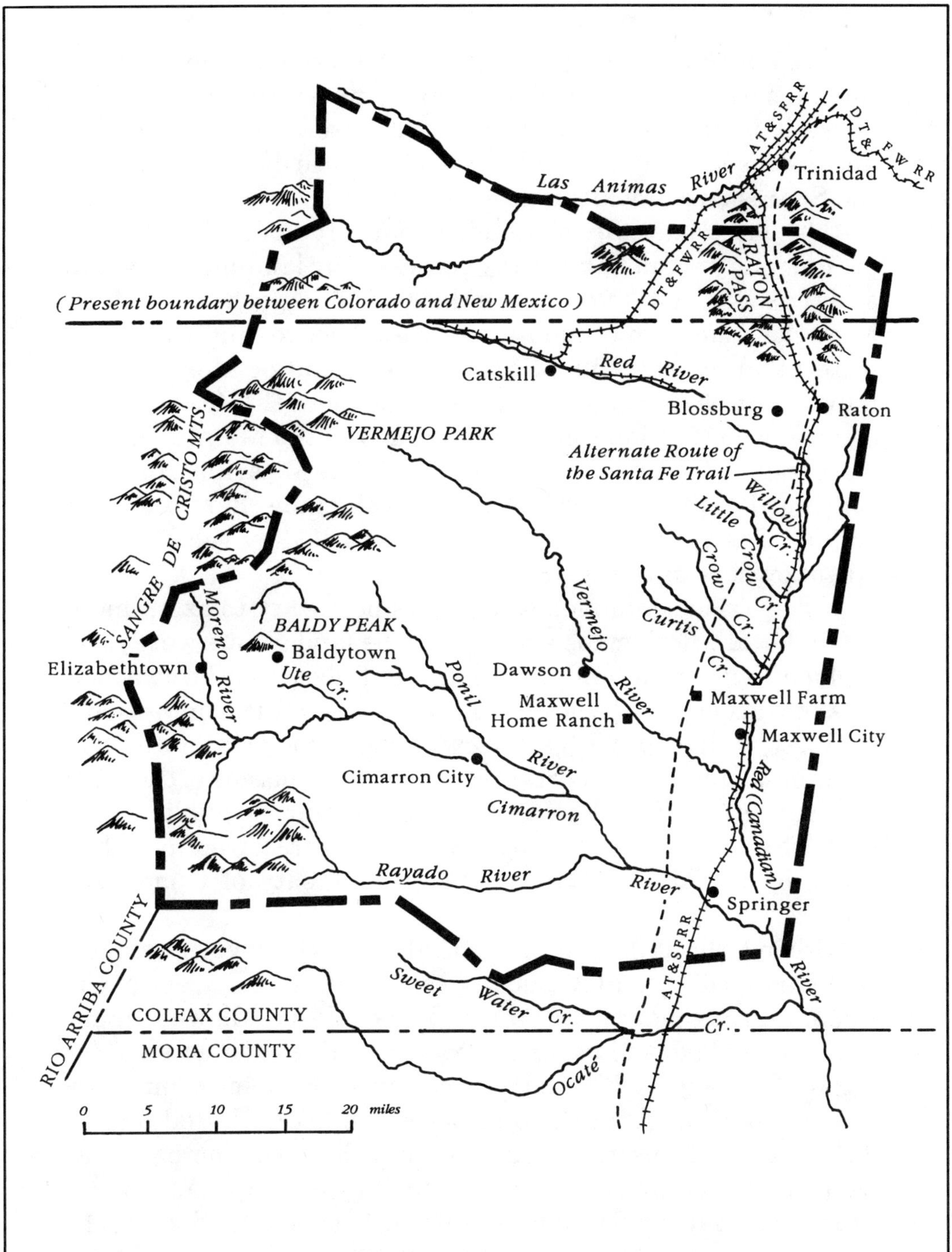

Map 8
Maxwell Land Grant in 1893

resulted in an excess payment to the Tribe. The issue of compensation of land grants remains important, however, because it is part of the history of the case and a part of the interesting history of the relations of the Jicarilla Apaches with the Spanish and Mexican governments.

The Tribe basically contended that large portions of land-grant lands were not physically possessed by land-grant owners and thus were not "taken" from the Jicarilla Apaches until long after the American occupation of New Mexico, and then they were taken by the United States, not Spain or Mexico. The tribal attorneys could not understand how the Commission could decide that land-grant lands such as the Maxwell Grant were taken by Spain and Mexico as the Jicarilla Apaches continued to plant crops and hunt small game there until the 1870s. Their "occupancy" was not disturbed by the Maxwell Grant owners until the 1880s.

The Tribe contended that it was necessary to examine in great detail whether the acreages of the land grants were to be included within the lands for which the Tribe was to be awarded compensation. The Tribe presented three separate contentions.

First, with respect to seven town grants, the Tribe contended that the common-land portions of the grants, outside of the town allotments, remained in the public domain as public lands under Spanish and Mexican law and were received as public lands by the United States under the Treaty of Guadalupe Hidalgo.

Second, the Tribe contended that the U.S. surveyor general had surveyed several Mexican private grants in excess of the maximum acreage per grantee that could be allowed under applicable Mexican law, or in excess of the explicit acreage set out in the grant itself, and that such excess acreage comprised, in fact, public lands at the time of cession to the United States. The essence of this argument was that the excess acreage was taken by the United States rather than by the Mexican government and that the Tribe was entitled to compensation for the excess acreage. The common town grants contained 1,658,765 acres, and the excessively surveyed Mexican private land grants had 2,798,193 acres, totaling 4,456,958 acres of public lands surveyed and patented to the grantees by the United States. These lands should have formed a basis for which the Tribe would have been entitled to compensation.

Finally, a third contention was made by the Tribe concerning 282,127 acres not used by the grantees. Jicarilla Apache bands continued in their usual way of life throughout the period of Spanish and Mexican sovereignty, because there was no use by the grantees during the Spanish or Mexican periods. They continued to use and occupy the lands until they were placed on their reservation.

The following analysis was presented to the Commission with respect to land-grant acreage:

1. Invalid Baca Location No. 2 Grant according to stipulation—52,109 acres.
2. Acreage of common areas of town grants that remained in the public domain subject to Indian property rights prior to cession—1,658,765 acres.
3. Acreage of Mexican private land grants in excess of original grant or of legal maximum of 11 leagues that were public domain subject to Indian property rights prior to cession—2,798,193 acres.
4. Other acreage not shown by evidence of United States to have been divested of Indian title and possession prior to cession—282,127 acres.

Total acreage of surveyed land grant acreages to be included in awarded lands—4,791,194 acres.

Total acreage shown by evidence to have been taken from Indian title and rights of possession prior to cession—68,382 acres.

The Tribe contended that under Spanish and Mexican law, mineral rights in granted lands remained in the government, unless the grant stated otherwise, and that none of the grants in the award area so stated.

Conclusion

The Tribe argued unsuccessfully before the Indian Claims Commission that the grantees within the claim area, whether individuals or towns recognized by the Spanish and Mexican governments, could not take these lands from the Indians until they were placed on the reservation, except for those parts of the granted land which were actually settled or used by grantees or by settlers within the town grants.

Unfortunately the Commission had previously decided in similar cases that Indian title had been extinguished by the prior sovereigns (Spain and Mexico) and that these lands never became a part of the public domain of the United States. Therefore the United States had no liability for acts of the prior sovereigns, which may have committed the acts that led to the extinguishment of the title. However, the attorneys for the Tribe believed that the earlier cases (not involving New Mexico grants) would be overruled by the Commission.

The Commission's opinion with respect to land grants, 17 I.C.C. 338, 409 (1966), stated as follows:

> The petitioners have presented impressive and voluminous documentary and other evidence and testimony seeking to overturn the long line of decisions in which this Commission has consistently held that the validity of confirmed Spanish and Mexican land grants cannot be questioned.
>
> The defendant has consistently maintained and presented evidence and testimony to support its position, that the United States cannot be held liable with respect to land grants already declared valid by the Congress or the Court of Private Land Claims; and that the validity and extent of confirmed land grants has already been determined by a body vested with judicial capacity, and cannot be re-examined by this Commission.
>
> Counsel for both parties presented this phase of the proceeding in great depth. We have given careful study of and serious consideration to the provocative and illuminating testimony of the experts, the careful selection of relevant

documentary evidence and the learned and excellently prepared proposed findings and briefs of the parties.

In brief, the position of the petitioner is that the fundamental Indian aboriginal rights of use and occupancy were not divested by the Mexican and Spanish land grants; that such rights were divested only to the extent that the grantees took physical possession of same; and that the said grants were made by Spain and Mexico subject to the Indian title and rights of use and occupancy.

The defendant contends these questions are stare decisis, and cites a number of cases in which the Commission has considered and ruled on these questions in matters involving other areas which were, as in this case, ceded to the United States by Mexico by the Treaty of Guadalupe Hidalgo, February 2, 1848 (9 Stat. 922).

After a careful study and evaluation of the record herein, we are of the opinion that the evidence and testimony does not justify a variance from the position which this Commission has previously taken in matters involving these issues relating to Mexican and Spanish land grants. . . .

We, therefore, hold that the Indian title to the lands embraced within the award area described in Finding No. 60 herein which were in the areas of the confirmed Spanish and Mexican land grants (see our Findings 64 and 65, supra) was extinguished by the prior sovereign and not by the defendant; that these lands never became a part of the public domain of the defendant; and that the defendant has no liability for any tortious acts of the prior sovereigns which may have been committed in the acts which led to the extinguishment of said title. In the Cochiti case (supra), we expressed our opinion on the various facets of this issue at length.

8

• • •

DATES OF TAKING AND VALUATION

The use and occupancy of the award area of the Jicarilla Apaches from the date of the occupation of New Mexico by the United States prior to 1883 was established by Dr. Thomas's testimony, with particular reference to the historical materials documenting contacts between the Jicarilla Apaches, government agents, and the military during the period.

Dr. Hibben's testimony clearly established that the Jicarilla Apaches had hunted, gathered, and farmed throughout portions of the award area from time immemorial. The archaeological evidence presented by Dr. Hibben in his testimony before the Commission in 1964 showed that this use and occupancy continued during the American period throughout the claim area until 1887, when the Jicarilla Apaches were finally placed on their present reservation.

Jicarilla Campsites and Settlements

When Dr. Hibben accompanied the informant Juan Dedios on hunting expeditions in 1933 and 1934, he identified sites at which the Jicarilla Apaches had lived and hunted from time immemorial. In 1958 he retraced his earlier explorations and based his identification of these sites upon the existing evidence of distinctive Jicarilla Apache houses, pottery, tools, and settlement patterns.

Of the roughly three hundred sites located in the original claim area, about eighty were established as unquestionably Jicarilla; others were probably Jicarilla, but this could not be demonstrated absolutely. The villages and campsites shown in map 4 are sites absolutely identified as Jicarilla Apache sites.

In the 1958 hearing, Dr. Hibben did not attempt to date the use of these sites exactly. However, between the first hearing and that of 1964, Dr. Hibben made an additional study of these sites and the objects found in them, revisiting a number of them to verify his findings and to obtain additional materials.

Although pottery is not helpful for exact dating purposes, because it was continually used from prehistoric times, Dr. Hibben did find items that could be dated, such as glass of various sorts, which could be dated to within a decade. Trade beads could be fairly closely dated under certain conditions; excavated brass cartridges from the time when fixed ammunition came into use could be dated exactly in some cases, as could pieces of brass, if they could be identified as part of a gun or other manufactured item.

These materials were used in connection with data obtained from informants and documentary materials in the record in order to date the use of these sites within fairly narrow limits. For example Juan Dedios would indicate that he camped at a particular site in about 1870, and Dr. Hibben would look for materials that might be dated at that particular site. In examining the historical materials from the various Jicarilla Apache sites within the award area, Dr. Hibben directed his attention to material deposited after the Civil War, primarily in the late 1860s and 1870s.

In the 1964 hearing, Dr. Hibben discussed various sites that were shown on the map introduced into evidence; proceeding in a counter-clockwise direction from the southwestern corner (near Moriarty), he described the sites one by one (map 4).

Investigations of Particular Sites

The Moriarty sites are located at the northern end of the Estancia Valley; the area was identified to Dr. Hibben by Juan Dedios as an antelope-hunting area. The sites are listed on map 2 as numbers 75 (Lobo Hill), 76 (Stanley site), 77 (Crow Butte), and 79 (Bald Hill). Crow Butte (plate 17) is typical of the area;

it is a prominent mesa about 100 feet high, considered a favorite camping site not only by Juan Dedios but also by another informant, James Garfield Velarde. Both Dedios and Velarde had camped and hunted on this site before and after the Civil War.

When the site was examined again in 1958, tipi-pole skeletons were still standing on the site, which indicated that they were used until the Jicarillas were taken to their present reservation in 1887. At this site Dr. Hibben found pieces of brass and portions of beer bottles, identified by Dr. Arthur Woodward of the Southwest Museum as being a type made about 1870. By the time the Indians came into possession of the the bottles, which they used for carrying water and other domestic purposes, it would have been later in the 1870s.

Dr. Hibben found a 44-caliber shell, a center-fire cartridge from a Henry repeating rifle, which came into use about 1866. It was presumed that by the time the Indians received these rifles, it would probably have been the 1880s. He also found a large number of tipi rings at these sites, from prehistoric ones buried as deep as 3 feet underground up to, and overlapping, those from modern times. Using these materials and his general collection of historical materials, Dr. Hibben concluded that these Moriarty sites were continuously occupied as late as the 1880s.

Dr. Hibben placed the use of the Crow Butte site after the 1860s because of the comments of Juan Dedios that not only was the site used extensively after the "great war," but that it was used for antelope hunting, which continued to be "very good" until the Circle-Dot Ranch took over the area about 1885. Because it was hard to find good game areas, and because this was one of the best antelope-hunting areas for the Jicarillas, the Crow Butte sites remained important for such hunting in the 1870s.

The Tecolote site is near the town of Tecolote, New Mexico, in the central portion of the award area; it is identified as site 80 on map 4. It is a very extensive site with considerable archaeological evidence; it was pointed out to Dr. Hibben by his informants. The site contained a number of buildings of a type usually used in the more permanent settlements, including sweathouses and hogans. Here was undoubtedly the site used as a base for trading with nearby Pecos Pueblo, as indicated by a number of historical references. Some of the early informants also stated that they had lived at Tecolote and south of Pecos, near Anton Chico, when they were trading with Pecos Pueblo.

At Tecolote Dr. Hibben found brass cartridge cases, which were used to show that the Jicarillas occupied this site after United States sovereignty, since the Spanish did not allow them to keep firearms. References already in the record indicated that the Jicarillas were well-armed with firearms in the 1870s and early 1880s. The evidence included fixed ammunition with brass cartridge shells, which did not come into use until the end of the Civil War; this type was not introduced into the West to any extent until after the war had ended. He also found several brass cartridge cases of 40-60 caliber shells, which were fired in military carbines no earlier than the 1870s. Dr. Hibben concluded that there was abundant information on the Tecolote site indicating that it was used from prehistoric times up to and including the 1870s and 1880s and that this use was continuous and regular from year to year.

The Tecolote site served as a good example of a very large site that evidenced continued use. Some of the materials were deeply buried, while others overlapped in a continuous sequence, with no sterile stratum or other evidence that the site had been abandoned at any time.

In the southeast corner of the award area are the Ima sites (site 64, map 4), some of the largest sites in this area. These sites were pointed out to Dr. Hibben by Juan Dedios as regular camping places. Dr. Hibben noticed several hundred tipi rings at these sites, which are located on the Llano Estacado, or Staked Plains. On the northeast side of the location was a protected area where the Jicarillas could get wood and water and find protection from unwanted visitors. From here they found easy access to the buffalo-hunting areas, where the southern herd moved north and south along the line between New Mexico and Texas.

In excavating the Ima sites, Dr. Hibben found historical material such as pottery and stone implements in the deeper diggings. In the upper levels, he found identifiable items such as glass bottles and brass cartridge shells, which the Jicarillas often used for carrying pollen and also as decoration for their buckskin shirts and pants. The brass cartridges were identified in most cases as post-Civil War; it would have been the 1870s by the time the Jicarillas received them. Dr. Hibben also found chinaware of American manufacture, which would date the sites as being occupied after the Civil War.

These sites were also located on a major trail that led to the Bosque Largo and Bosque Redondo and to the trail to the Mescalero Reservation, to which the government had several times attempted unsuccessfully to remove the Jicarillas. They were very large sites and contained considerable archaeological evidence that in the 1870s several hundred lodges and tipis were located there. Dr. Hibben concluded that the Jicarillas continued to use this area in the 1870s and early 1880s, and he could find no evidence of an interruption of use by the Jicarillas during the latter half of the nineteenth century.

There were several sites near the present town of San Jon, two of which are listed on map 4 as sites 66 and 67, in the southeastern corner of the award area, at the edge of the Llano Estacado. Dr. Hibben definitely identified these two sites as Jicarilla sites from the pottery and permanent house types. He dated the latest use of these sites as post–Civil War, based on several brass center-fire cartridge shells of various calibers found there.

Site 66 was described by Juan Dedios as one of the best areas for hunting buffalo, because the buffalo migration took place along the Llano Estacado, and the Jicarillas could practically see the buffalo herds from this camp. Dedios said that he had camped and hunted from this site after the Civil War.

The Ritter Crossing site (number 68, map 4) is located east of Logan, New Mexico, on the Canadian River, in the east-southeastern portion of the award area. Here the buffalo herds crossed the Canadian River; it was a famous hunting area. Dr. Hibben also found evidence here that the site was used after the Civil War.

A large number of sites on Ute Creek (numbers 57–61, map 4) were shown to Dr. Hibben by Juan Dedios and were also mentioned by James Garfield Velarde in his deposition. These sites were on a major trail that led from the center of the award area, in the vicinity of Mora, eastward to the buffalo-hunting plains; they were in a more or less protected area, near an abundance of water.

These were permanent sites, with evidence of many permanent habitations still visible. All were located within one or two days' march of the buffalo-hunting area to the east. At site 61, Dr. Hibben excavated from a house site a brass cartridge case from a 40-60 caliber center-fired rifle that he dated as being manufactured after 1870. This evidence futher established the later occupancy date.

Dr. Hibben concluded that sites 60 and 61 were regularly occupied by the Jicarilla Apaches until the demise of the buffalo herds in 1883. There was no interruption of Jicarilla use of these sites evident in the archaeological record, but rather the complete sequences indicated continued use and occupancy by a large number of Jicarillas during their annual hunts.

The Dead Man's Mesa sites, shown as site numbers 53, 54, and 55 (map 4; see also plate 10) in the east-central portion of the award area, are spectacular sites, located on isolated mesas. They were first shown to Dr. Hibben by Juan Dedios, and were used extensively after the Civil War. These sites were also known to Velarde, who indicated that he had hunted there as a young man throughout the 1870s and early 1880s. Permanent buildings were located on top of these mesas, especially on Dead Man's Mesa. There is only one means of access to the top of this mesa (through a small crack with artificial handholds), so that it could easily be defended from enemies. From the site on Dead Man's Mesa, the buffalo herds were visible 20 to 30 miles to the east; it was the terminus of one of the Apache trails that led eastward from the Mora area.

Excavations at this site by Dr. Hibben uncovered a continuity of occupation by its inhabitants and an abundance of historical material. For instance, he was able to identify pieces of glass he found (such as a beer bottle made in St. Louis) as being made after 1870. Through such evidence he concluded that these sites were continuously occupied by the Jicarillas until 1883 or 1884.

The Rabbit Ear Mountain area, in the northeastern section of the award area, contains sites number 82, 83, 84, 87, 88, and 89 (map 4). Juan Dedios, Alasco Tisnado, and James Garfield Velarde had all lived at these sites and hunted from them. Some of the informants stated that they were born in this area, indicating that the sites served as permanent camps. The Jicarillas could see the entire northeastern boundary of the award area from here and could hunt different kinds of game (buffalo, mountain sheep, and elk) throughout the northeastern portion of the award area from the sites.

At site 84, along a tributary of Rabbit Ear Creek, Dr. Hibben excavated an abundance of archaeological material, finding more cartridge cases dated to the 1870s and 1880s. He was able to corroborate his own excavations with a considerable amount of historical material found by a local collector near these sites. His excavations revealed level after level of tipi rings and, in some cases, more permanent habitations, such as sweatlodges. The debris indicated continuous occupation by the Jicarillas, especially from the period after the Civil War (probably the 1870s).

Dr. Hibben concluded, based on his own investigation, that these sites were occupied continuously from the first American occupation up to and even after 1883. This conclusion was strengthened by evidence that these sites formed a major complex of buffalo-hunting sites, so that their last occupation was probably 1883 or 1884.

Tramperos Creek, site number 67 (map 4), is located in the east-central portion of the award area. Here Dr. Hibben found considerable historical material, including pieces of a brass canteen known to date from the Civil War, which most likely would have appeared at the site sometime after the end of the war.

The Trinchera Pass site number 73 (map 4), east of Raton, New Mexico, was shown to Dr. Hibben by Juan Dedios, who indicated that it was a major Jicarilla camping place on the way north to hunting grounds in the northern regions of the Arkansas River. This site is located near the natural passageway through the range of the mountains that swings eastward from Raton.

Juan Dedios said that he had camped there after the Civil War, when he used the trail north to hunt the northern buffalo and elk. Dr. Hibben concluded that this campsite and trail (the major trail into the northern hunting grounds) were regularly used until 1883, when the buffalo herds that normally ranged through southeastern Colorado disappeared.

In the Cimarron area, in the north-central and northwest-central portions of the award area, sites 71A, 71B, and 72 (map 4) were also shown to Dr. Hibben by Juan Dedios. Cimarron was a ration-distribution point opened in 1861, and there were many indications that there were forty to fifty campsites situated in this region. Historical materials recovered here revealed that the Jicarillas had lived and farmed in the vicinity from 1861 to 1878.

Jicarilla Trails

The major trails used by the Jicarillas during the American period within the award area are shown on map 4. These trails were pointed out to Dr. Hibben by Juan Dedios. In addition Dr. Hibben went over portions of these trails with Garfield Velarde.

One of the major trails, T-10, led from Mora, located in the west-central portion of the award area, in a southeasterly direction to Trementina, across the Canadian River in the vicinity of Conchas Lake. From there it proceeded down the Canadian River to the campsites at Ima and San Jon.

Another major trail, T-3, started from the Rio Grande, passed through the Eagle Nest area and on to Cimarron, then went in an easterly and northeasterly direction through the northeastern portion of the award area along the Cimarron River. Then it continued eastward to the buffalo-hunting grounds in northeastern New Mexico and southeastern Colorado.

A major branch of one of these trails, T-2, proceeded from the west-central portion of the award area, in the vicinity of Mora, in a northerly direction to the Canadian Crossing. Then it passed to the east through the middle portion of the award area. From there it continued on to Dead Man's Mesa, in the east-central portion of the award area. Another branch led in a southeasterly direction to the Ute Creek sites.

These trails were generally connected to major village and camping sites of the Jicarilla Apaches. Dr. Hibben concluded that they were used continually by the Jicarillas from early times up to the date when they discontinued buffalo hunting, as corroborated by his aged informants.

Jicarilla Sacred Places

There are a number of locations within the award area that the Jicarillas regarded as sacred places in their hunting expeditions. In the southeastern portion of the award area was Tucumcari Butte, where the Jicarillas touched the stone before going to hunt. Rabbit Ear Mountain, in the northeast, was pointed out by Juan Dedios and mentioned by Garfield Velarde, who as a boy, after the Civil War, laid his hands on a certain stone before going buffalo hunting. The Sierra Grande, a prominent volcanic cone in the northeast, was a place where the spirits dwelled, according to Velarde. Both of the men mentioned that there was hunting there after the Civil War.

Sierra Blanca in Colorado (plate 15) was a place where they hunted elk and mountain sheep after the Civil War, according to the testimony of several of the older informants. It was considered a place that was close to the sky and the spirits. The Spanish Peaks, a series of peaks situated south of Walsenburg, Colorado, were also sacred places, mentioned by the informants Tisnado, Velarde, Dedios, and Luna Vicenti as locations that were visited every year by members of the Tribe.

The Depositions of Jicarilla Elders

Place of birth is very important to a Jicarilla Apache. In the depositions of July 27, 1953, several of the informants related where they were born. This was important to the case, because place of birth indicated that the site was, at the time, a permanent camp, since births did not take place in temporary hunting camps.

Tex K. Baldine, more than 80 years old in 1953, was born at Agua Fria, in the Oklahoma panhandle, in the extreme northeastern portion of the award area. Sixto Atole, of the same age, stated that he was born east of Cimarron. Their birth dates would have been between 1870 and 1880. Sixto also related that as a young man he had gone on buffalo hunts along the Arkansas River.

Woodhall Quintana, 83 years old in 1953, was born at Cimarroncita, a side canyon of the Cimarron River, near the town of Cimarron. Quintana stated that he had hunted regularly east of the Canadian River in the area known as Dead Man's Mesa, in the east-central portion of the award area, and had camped there as a young man.

Garfield Velarde, who was 101 years old at the time he gave his deposition in 1953, stated that he was born on the Conejos River (see plates 19–20). He told of extensive hunts east of the river when he was a young man, during which camps near the Rabbit Ear Mountain were used. Velarde also told of using trails and hunting and camping in the vicinity of Bueyeros, Dead Man's Mesa, and the sites near Gallegos on Ute Creek.

John M. Baltazar, 74 years old in 1953, was born near Raton, in the north-central portion of the award area. His testimony was consistent with that of the other elders.

Dr. Hibben's Conclusions

Based on archaeological, anthropological, and historical evidence, and citing information received from informants and others pertinent to the investigation, Dr. Hibben concluded that the Jicarilla Apaches continued in possession and use of the award area, in accord with their usual way of life, from prehistoric times through the Spanish and Mexican periods and throughout the American period until about 1883, the last year of the migration of the southern buffalo herd.

Following the sudden demise of the herd, which was the major game animal of the Jicarillas in the eastern part of the award area, they no longer had any reason to hunt there. In addition, in August of 1883, the Jicarillas were effectively removed to Fort Stanton, on the Mescalero Reservation in south-central New Mexico. This event significantly altered the pattern of life that had persisted remarkably well all during the previous attempts to remove the Tribe from the claim area.

Dr. Hibben concluded that there was relatively little interference with the usual Jicarilla pattern of living and use and occupancy of the claim area by reason of any settlement of the area by non-Indians, including those of Mexican and Spanish origin, until 1883. Non-Indian cultivation involved a very small percentage of the award area. These lands were clustered around Las Vegas, a small area in the Pecos River Valley, in the Tecolote River Valley, and in the Cimarron area. The existence of these cultivated areas did not interfere with the use and occupancy of the Jicarillas in the remaining portions of the award area, according to their aboriginal pattern of hunting and gathering.

In general Dr. Hibben was unaware of any interference with Jicarilla use and occupancy of the land-grant areas within the award area by reason of their use by grantees and other non-

Plate 19
James Garfield Velarde, ca. 1890s
(courtesy Smithsonian Institution National Anthropological Archives)

Indians. In fact there is no evidence of abandonment by the Jicarillas of any of the award area or land-grant areas until 1883. To the contrary the Jicarillas continued to occupy these areas, which they considered to be their own (regardless of whether they were on land grants), and they did so into the early 1880s.

Plate 20
Ed Ladd, Emmet Wirt,
and James Garfield Velarde,
Lumberton, N.M., 1896

(courtesy Smithsonian Institution National Anthropological Archives)

They continued their annual buffalo hunts and other hunting-and-gathering activities until that time, as evidenced by the materials found in their tipi sites and other hunting sites, datable to the American period.

Although a ration point was established at Cimarron in 1861, it provided only a very small part of the livelihood of the Jicarillas. Cimarron was one of several places where agencies or subagencies were established by the government from time to time and where rations and other supplies could be furnished to Indians, generally by Indian agents. The Apaches could not stay within the Cimarron area without supplemental food supplies, so they grew crops in the vicinity and relied upon gathering and hunting expeditions. The buffalo hunt was one of their most important sources of food.

Reports by Indian agents and the military, also cited by Dr. Hibben, supported his conclusions; the Commission based its findings in part on these records.

The Evidence of Township Surveys

Dr. Leroy Gordon, the tribe's expert in geography, prepared a map of the award area that showed the dates of the U.S. surveyor general's township-survey plats and field notes of the area, including wire fences; the same map also recorded the evidence of use, improvements, and occupancy indicated on the plats and notes (map 7).

The purpose of this evidence was to establish that there was very little settlement of the award area and that the Jicarilla Apaches were not deprived of its use and occupancy or prevented from engaging in their hunting-and-gathering activities there.

These township-survey plats were 6 miles by 6 miles in size, except for a few incomplete townships. Each survey plat was a detailed map, and most of the plats were accompanied by a set of surveyor's notes. These plats and notes covered townships in the award area for ranges numbered from 7 north to 31 north, inclusive (from a line south of Interstate 40 northward to a line just south of the Colorado border).

The notes generally included a description of the boundaries of each township and a comment on the character of the terrain, the slope, the surface-forming materials, natural vegetation, and improvements in the township area. Dr. Gordon obtained surveys of every township in the award area, with the exception of eight or nine that he indicated by question marks.

The great majority of the township surveys and land entries were made under the Homestead Act and the Desert Land Act. The five-year Homestead Act permitted settlers to enter a claim for a maximum of 160 acres of either surveyed or unsurveyed public lands. Settlers were entitled to a patent after they had constructed a habitable house and cultivated part of the claim or lived on it for five years, at which time the patent could be reduced to ownership by cash payment.

The U.S. surveyor general did not comment on the number of years a habitation had been present, but since a person making a claim to a homestead had to spend five years on the 160 acres before patenting it, a date five years previous to the survey request for patent appeared to be a reasonable date for the first entry by that person. Although an individual did not have to patent the claim as soon as possible, it would be logical, as the land was becoming valuable, for a settler to patent the land after only five years.

The U.S. surveyor general of New Mexico established a north-south line in the Rio Grande Valley and an east-west line close to the mouth of the Rio Puerco at a place called San Marcial, with directions as to the type of marker to be used. Following establishment of these meridian and base lines, a series of east-west and north-south lines at six-mile intervals was established across the award area.

The subdivision into blocks of 36 square miles began within the individual townships, under contract with the settlers. The surveyor examined the entirety of each township and normally had several weeks to make a survey of the 36 square miles within the township. He could cover it all on horseback in some detail.

A sketch map of New Mexico by the U.S. surveyor general, dated 1862, showed grants in the award area, such as the Las Vegas, Preston Beck, and Anton Chico grants; the Mora Grant and the Antonio Ortiz Grant were not shown. The map shows the Jicarilla Apaches located in the general area of the Maxwell Grant (the grant itself was not indicated on the map), across the award area west of the Canadian River. No settlements are shown east of the Canadian in this survey map. Another survey map, dated 1876, showed the Mora and Pablo Montoya grants for the first time.

An 1879 map of New Mexico showed the Antonio Ortiz and Maxwell grants for the first time. It also showed that the eastern portion of the award area had been covered by exterior boundary lines and that a number of townships had been subdivided. There was no extensive settlement in the portion of the award area east of the Canadian River; a number of place names appeared, but they were names of natural features. In the western part of the award area, a number of settlements were shown with Spanish names, but no settlement was recorded in the southwestern portion of the award area.

The Wheeler Survey was a land-classification map of a part of central New Mexico. It was unique for that time, because it was both detailed and showed the topography accurately. It was prepared for purposes of land planning and showed roadways and settlements in detail, along with towns, terrain, and potential land use. This survey also indicated that there was no significant settlement of any sort east of the Canadian River in those years.

The purpose of the surveys represented by the maps of the U.S. surveyor general was to make lands in the public domain available and to establish a grid for the location of homestead claims. The exterior boundaries were carried across lands assumed to be public domain in preparing for homesteading.

Dr. Gordon did not know of any instances where the surveyor general had surveyed Spanish or Mexican land-grant lands. There was no reference to the Jicarilla Apaches in the surveyor general's maps, except that two of the sketches showed the Jicarillas in their usual general location, and an earlier one had shown the Jicarillas located well to the south, just north of Bosque Redondo.

Fencing would have been an obstacle to use on the award lands by the Jicarilla Apaches. However, prior to 1883, there was no fencing shown in the award area. The coming of the railroad to Albuquerque in 1880, accompanied by connections to Colorado and California in 1883, made barbed wire available in large quantities. Fencing was then extended rapidly throughout the territory.

The total number of townships in the award area was 477. Surveyed townships and land grants are shown on the map prepared by Dr. Gordon and admitted into evidence as Plantiff's Exhibit PL. G-4.

Townships represented by blank squares indicated no evidence of use, improvement, or occupancy at the time the particular township survey was made. Out of the 477 townships, the surveys of 165 recorded no land use, no improvements, and no occupancy. A shaded township square indicated a township stated by the surveyor to have been used only for grazing purposes, with no indication of habitation; 80 townships were so marked on his map.

There were also 245 townships that showed no indication of habitation within the survey area (51 percent of the total townships described).

The township surveys were so detailed that individual habitations could be accurately determined by Dr. Gordon. Seventy of the townships shown on the surveys included only one habitation for the entire area within the township. At the time the surveys were made, the typical structure was a small house, often with an adjoining corral.

No indications were given in the survey plats or notes of the number of cattle or the frequency of grazing within each shaded township. In addition grazing was indicated by shading an entire township, even though a very small portion might have been used for that purpose. Moreover the surveyors did not indicate whether the shaded townships were being used for grazing by Indians or non-Indians. However, Dr. Gordon presumed that grazing, largely of cattle, was being carried out by non-Indians, because the Jicarilla Apaches were not known to have grazed cattle in the area.

Patented Areas

There were 299 patents and cancellations in the award area up to 1881. The total acreage in these patents was approximately 0.5 percent of the total award area outside of the land grants, or a little less than 50 thousand acres out of almost 10 million acres.

Between 1881 and 1887, the total patents and cancellations increased to 1,252, representing 2.6 percent of the award area, excluding the grants. Of the total award area, including the grants, about 1.7 percent was patented or canceled by 1887.

Settlements

In 1807 all Spanish settlements near the award area were within the Rio Grande Valley, with the exception of Chilili and Pecos; only Pecos was actually within the award area.

Settlement east of the Rio Grande Valley proceeded very slowly. The first settlement was Mora, begun about 1818. The next settlement was Tecolote, in 1824. Anton Chico, Sangre de Cristo, and Las Vegas were settled about 1835. In 1841 a traveler in the area reported that there were no Mexican settlements north of Mora. However, evidence indicates that there was some slight settlement north of Mora at that time. Cimarron, in the Maxwell Grant (founded in 1841), is an example. As late as 1862, Anton Chico was spoken of as the first settlement to be encountered within New Mexico when coming westward from Camp Arbuckle.

In the survey plats and notes, the U.S. surveyor generally called any cluster of houses a settlement, especially in the eastern half of the award area, where normally only two or three houses were located together. For example the largest settlement east of the Canadian River was noted as having eight families. In the western part of the award area, the settlements were somewhat larger.

The Character of the Land

Cultivation was not practiced except in the northern part of the award area near Cimarron; less than 0.25 percent of the award area was under cultivation in 1880. Generally the area east of the Canadian and even some of the area to the west was grassland, used only for grazing at this time. The western part of the award area was predominantly sheep-grazing country, whereas the eastern settlement that had taken place five or six years before the surveys had resulted from the western movement of cattlemen.

Valuation Date

The Tribe argued that the date of taking (and therefore, valuation) occurred in the 1880s. Historical evidence included reports of contact by the military, government agents, and others with the Jicarilla Apaches. These incidents occurred during the years 1846 (the beginning of the American period) through 1879 and were more fully reported by Dr. Alfred B. Thomas.

The continued presence of the Jicarillas in Cimarron and throughout the award area continued to be of concern to government officials. On September 26, 1879, it was reported from Cimarron that five hundred Jicarillas who had resisted being moved to Fort Stanton were still there. The report continued, "The Indians were starving and killing cattle throughout the area, and they should be fed to prevent further trouble."

On November 26, 1879, Agent Benjamin. H. Thomas reported that a number of Jicarillas desired to go to Washington "with regard to getting a permanent home somewhere," and a delegation of Jicarillas made the trip in the spring of 1880. After this visit, on June 23, 1880 (see plate 21), the acting commissioner of Indian affairs directed Colonel F. B. Townsend to look

Plate 21
Jicarilla Apache Delegation to Washington, D.C., 1880

(courtesy Bureau of American Ethnology)

for a satisfactory location that would provide timber, a water supply, agricultural sites, and sufficient acreage for future allotments. He cautioned the agent to be careful not to select lands that would conflict with private grants known to be of mineral character, or upon which improvements had been made by whites. During this time the Jicarillas remained at Cimarron.

On September 11, the acting commissioner recommended to the secretary of the interior a location in Rio Arriba County, and on September 21, 1880, an executive order was issued establishing the reservation for the Jicarillas at the recommended location. The 1880 order was basically the same as the final executive order issued in 1887, which established the reservation that became the permanent home of the Tribe. However, the Jicarilla Apaches were not placed on the reservation provided by the 1880 executive order; instead they returned to Cimarron in the summer of 1881 and continued their usual activities in the award area.

On April 27, 1881, Agent Thomas reported, in part, that the reservation was being occupied by whites before the Indians could receive any benefit from it. He stated that one thousand settlers were already reported on the reserve, with more coming, and "I suspect if the Desert of Yuma were reserved for Indians it would immediately become invaluable and very desirable to the civilization. . . ."

The Jicarillas again returned to Cimarron and to their usual activities in the award area. Agent Thomas reported from Santa Fe on August 18, 1881, that:

> The tendency of the Jicarilla Apaches is toward Cimarron and they are glad of any pretext to go there. They may be there now for a visit, or it may be their intention to remain as long as possible. I do not believe there is any immediate danger of a conflict and as soon as I can find out how to accomplish the return of the Indians to their agency, I propose to take active measures for that purpose . . .

In October of 1881, the commissioner of Indian affairs directed Agent Thomas to move the Apaches to the new reservation as soon as possible, but the move was complicated by proposed action to move the Mescaleros to the new Jicarilla Apache Reservation. This was opposed by both the Jicarillas and the Mescaleros.

In December 1881 the Jicarillas were ordered to the new reservation, and the move began soon thereafter. The Jicarillas were located on the reservation in the spring of 1882; an act of Congress providing for consolidation of the Mescaleros with the Jicarillas on the new reservation west of the Rio Grande was opposed by the Mescaleros.

Shortly after the Jicarillas moved to the new reservation,

they once again left. Agent Thomas reported on July 11 that the Apaches were absent from the reservation; he found their camp about 6 miles east of Wagon Mound.

> Most of the men were out hunting, and while awaiting their return, we informed ourselves in regard to the camp. There were thirty-five lodges, representing about one-hundred-seventy-five Indians. The camp was well supplied with antelope meat and flour, and the Indians appeared to be in good condition.

Agent Thomas also reported that San Pablo and about twenty other men returned before night, bringing in plenty of game.

> In reply to my question of what he was doing San Pablo said he was out with a few of his people on a hunting expedition and he would move on further east down Red River and desire to reach the buffalo country; they wished to spend from two to four months in this way according to his success in finding game and would then return to the reservation . . .

It is clear that although a new reservation had been provided for the Apaches and they had moved there, they had left because they were not properly fed by the government. In 1883 the agent in charge of the reservation reported to the commissioner of Indian affairs that the population of the Jicarilla Apaches was 747 (see chart 5).

He reported that the Indians were late in receiving their annuities at their new reservation, forcing them to endure half of the exceedingly severe winter with practically no protection; they had to rely on their old tents or piles of brush of their own crude making for protection, buried in three-foot deep snows with temperatures dropping to 35° below zero. He again recommended they be removed to the Mescalero Reservation at Fort Stanton, where they could receive more aid from the government. In February 1883 Inspector C. H. Howard sent a letter to the secretary of the interior reviewing the situation and

Chart 5

Jicarilla Apache Population in 1883

Category	Number of Persons
Men	156
Women	230
Boys (of school age)	78
Girls (of school age)	49
Children (5 yrs./younger)	234
TOTAL	747

SOURCE: Annual Report, Commissioner of Indian Affairs, 1883, p.118

stating that the Mescaleros had no objection to sharing the reservation with the Jicarillas, so long as there was no trouble; they desired to have a delegation of Jicarillas come and inspect the reservation.

These recommendations were refused on the grounds of expense, which led to a great deal of dissatisfaction among the Jicarillas. Nevertheless the transport of the Jicarillas to Fort Stanton began again on August 20, 1883. They arrived on the Mescalero Reservation on October 9, 1883, after a trip marked by hardship, smallpox, and six deaths. The reservation that had been created for the Jicarillas west of the Rio Grande was returned to the public domain on May 15, 1884.

It was not long before the Jicarillas became dissatisfied with their location on the Mescalero Reservation. A number of them felt it was a waste of time to make permanent improvements, since they had no guarantee of being allowed to remain there, and they could not regard the reservation land as their own. They felt that they might be moved again at any time, at the will of the government. This move had been their fifth displacement during fifteen years. No land was ever assigned to the Jicarillas that could be considered acceptable for agriculture or irrigation, so the Jicarillas began to leave the Mescalero Reservation to return their old home once again.

In August of 1885, 260 of them were reported in the award area. On November 13, 1886, a report was received from General Nelson A. Miles, the military commander in Santa Fe, stating that the Jicarillas would rather die than go back to Fort Stanton. On November 23, 1886, the commanding officer there received a wire from the general in command at Santa Fe:

> Do not allow any more Jicarillas to leave reservation until after their case is settled in Washington, use all the force you have to prevent them, and make such disposition of troops as you consider advisable to compel them to remain.

Disregarding these orders, General Miles took up the matter directly with officials in Washington. Colonel Benjamin Grierson, who reported General Miles's mission, stated that:

> These Indians say they do not want to remain at the Mescalero Agency where the Mescalero have gotten everything, and they nothing, if they have to starve and freeze they prefer to do so elsewhere . . .

Increasing numbers of Jicarillas continued to leave Fort Stanton for the claim area. They requested that a reservation be established for them, their first choice being in the claim area, their second choice at the location of the reservation set aside for them west of the Rio Grande by the executive order of 1880. After investigation their second choice was recommended to Washington. In the meantime, the Jicarillas had been engaging in the hunt and other activities in the award area.

Pursuant to the request of the Jicarillas, and based on the recommendations of government officials, President Grover Cleveland issued an executive order dated February 11, 1887, setting forth a reservation that was essentially the northern half of the present Jicarilla Apache Reservation. The executive order read as follows:

> It is hereby ordered that all that portion of the public domain in the Territory of New Mexico which, when surveyed, will be embraced in the following townships, viz: 27, 28, 29, and 30 north, ranges 1 east, and 1, 2, and 3 west; 31

> and 32 north, ranges 2 and 3 west, and the south half of township 31 north, range 1 west, be, and the same is hereby, set apart as a reservation for the use and occupation of the Jicarilla Apache Indians provided: That this order shall not be so construed as to deprive any bona fide settler of any valid rights he may have acquired under the law of the United States providing for the disposition of the public domain.

Date of Valuation Becomes Date of Effective Removal

The year 1883 was the date of valuation (date of taking) proposed by the Tribe, which was the date the Tribe was effectively removed from use and possession of the award area. The attorneys for the Tribe argued that since there had been no treaty between the United States and the Tribe constituting a legal taking of the land, the rule for determining the date of valuation (or date of taking by the United States) was the date when the Tribe's use and occupancy of the award area was effectively eliminated, and the Tribe was deprived of and removed from the award area.

A prior case stating this rule was that of *Snake or Paiute Indians v. United States,* 4 I.C.C. 571 (1956), in which the Commission stated that the Indians were actually deprived of their possessory and occupancy rights "when they were removed from their land and placed on the Yakima Reservation." Similarly in the Spokane Tribe case, *Spokane Tribe of Indians v. United States,* 9 I.C.C. 236 (1961), the Commission stated that:

> Since the 1887 agreement [under which the Commission found that the entire tribe had agreed to remove to the Coeur d'Alene Reservation in Idaho] by its terms became effective July 13, 1892, that being the date of its ratification, that date becomes the date of taking of all land outside the reservation area.

This doctrine was approved by the Supreme Court of the United States in *U.S. v. Santa Fe Pacific R.R. Co.,* 314 U.S. 339

(1941), where the Court said, at page 358:

> In view of the long-standing attempt to settle the Walapais' problem by placing them on a reservation, their acceptance of this reservation must be regarded in law as the equivalent of a release of any tribal rights which they may have had in lands outside the reservation.

The 1883 date was in fact approved by the Commission as the date of taking.

The testimony of Dr. Hibben, considered with the documentary evidence submitted at the previous hearing, supported by the testimony of Dr. Leroy Gordon, established conclusively that the Jicarillas had continued their use and occupancy of the entire award area, without substantial interruption, from earliest times to the American occupation, until the year 1883. Dr. Hibben's testimony with regard to this continuous use and occupancy was not contradicted by the United States, but was supported by the written reports of Indian agents and military personnel, as compiled by the Stanford Research Institute and quoted by Dr. Thomas and Dr. Hibben.

The Commission nevertheless limited the area claimed by the Tribe (map 6). Although the evidence for occupation of the entire claimed area was convincing in the view of the attorneys for the Tribe, the Commission reduced the award without explanation. It is difficult to avoid the conclusion that the commissioners simply were of the opinion that too few would be getting too much.

Findings and Opinion of the Commission

The conclusions of the Commission were set forth in its findings numbered 166 to 168, 17 I.C.C. 338, 403:

> **166.** Based on the archeological, anthropological and historical evidence and the information received from informants and others, we find that the Jicarilla Apaches continued in possession and usage of the award area according to their usual way of life from prehistoric times

through the Spanish and Mexican periods and through the American period into the 1880s. The migration of the southern buffalo herd ceased in 1883. Following this sudden killing off of the buffalo herd, which was the major game animal of the Jicarillas in the eastern part of the award area, an important reason for being there was gone.

167. The date upon which the United States, without payment of compensation and in the absence of a ratified treaty of cession with the Jicarilla Apache Tribe, took from that tribe its Indian title to lands within the State of New Mexico which it had used and occupied since time immemorial, and as set out in our Finding No. 60 herein, (excluding confirmed Spanish and Mexican land grants), was August 20, 1883, the date the U.S. Army began its removal of these Indians to Fort Stanton.

It is true, as we have found above, that these Indians reluctantly went to Fort Stanton; that conditions there were unfavorable, and, in fact, incompatible to their continued presence there; that they had to continue their old way of life for part of their subsistence while at Stanton; and that many of them escaped to return to the award area in 1886. However, the move carried out by the military, starting on August 20, 1883, to Fort Stanton resulted in a sufficient disruption of their way of life and interference with their overall use and occupancy of their lands (see Finding 60, ante) to constitute an extinguishment of their title thereto.

This disruption continued for approximately three years before a number of the Jicarillas escaped and returned to the award area, there to pursue their old way of life over a portion of that area and on a limited scale. This disruption was substantial in character and time as distinguished from the prior brief but unsuccessful attempts to place these Indians on reservations.

To this it is relevant to find that although the Fort Stanton reservation was not one of their choice, these Indians had sent a delegation to Washington several years before and had requested a reservation; that after their placement at

> Fort Stanton they requested the reservation which was created by the Executive Order of February 11, 1887, which is virtually the same one created by the 1880 Executive Order; and that they voluntarily moved thereon in 1887 and have lived there ever since.
>
> **168.** The Commission finds that the plaintiff is entitled to recover of and from the defendant for and on behalf of the Jicarilla Apache Tribe of Indians the fair market value of the lands described in Finding of Fact No. 60 as we have herein designated same to exclude the confirmed Spanish and Mexican Land Grants (see our Findings of Fact Nos. 64 and 65) as of August 20, 1883, less such offsets, if any, to which defendant may be entitled under the provisions of the Indian Claims Commission Act (60 Stat. 1049).

The Indian Claims Commission issued its opinion on the issue of land grants and the date of valuation on November 9, 1966. It reviewed prior proceedings and considered first the issue of land grants. That part of the opinion is set forth on pp. 115–16 above.

The Commission next considered the date of valuation (the date on which the Jicarillas lost their lands), the date the United States "took" these lands, and the date on which the fair value of the land would be determined. The Commission said, on pages 6–9 of its opinion, 17 I.C.C. 411:

> The documentary evidence and testimony presented in this supplemental proceeding has provided a sufficient basis for our final determination of the date of taking. Since there was never a treaty of cession of the said lands and since the early Executive Order Reservations, through no fault on the part of these Indians, proved to be merely abortive attempts to provide the Jicarillas with a permanent home, it has been necessary for us to determine the date of extinguishment of Indian title on the basis of disruption and deprivation.
>
> We have, therefore, made detailed Findings of Fact numbered 69 through 168 which reflect the chronological historical facts of record and the application of the scientific

techniques of the fields of applied geography and anthropology in an effort to determine the degree of confirmation of these through documentary and other acceptable and reliable records.

In this, we have been fortunate in having available, field investigations made by Dr. Hibben in 1933 and 1934, a number of years prior to the institution of this litigation. His findings at that time were made wholly without the instant litigation in mind. He was also fortunate in having for his assistance and information aged Jicarilla Indians, who personally lived and experienced the Jicarilla way of life in the award area during the relative period after the Civil War. Dr. Hibben, a distinguished authority in his field, supplemented the information thus received by field investigations and excavations on which he was assisted by these informants. Thus, he was able to confirm their statements. These efforts were supplemented by further field investigations and excavations made by Dr. Hibben in 1958, after he had contracted with the petitioner to do so and to appear as he has at the proceedings before the Commission as an expert witness.

In our Findings numbered 81-98, we have detailed the facts which have been found from the information provided by the aged Jicarilla informants as they have been, in accordance with the requirements and standards of the archeological profession, confirmed through the said investigations and excavations of Dr. Hibben. These findings also detail the facts resulting from Dr. Hibben's studies and investigations, independent of the information received from these informants. Dr. Hibben's testimony was, in substance, as a mosaic, formed through the woven fabric of all of his sources of information.

This mosaic, as presented by Dr. Hibben, reflects the relevant detailing of the areas of use and occupation by the Jicarillas. It reflected the camp sites, the geographical location of game for the hunt, plants for the gathering and the sacred places for worship, trails and other relevant details of use and occupation. Even general indications of

> the period of use and occupation after the Civil War were developed which have been of particular value to us in our assessment of other evidentiary material in the record in this matter.
>
> Dr. Leroy Gordon, an expert in the field of applied geography, testified for the petitioner. We have detailed the facts we have found in this particular phase of our overall factual consideration in our Findings of Fact numbered 99-122.
>
> Briefly stated, we have found that during the relevant period surveys were made in the award area by the defendant prior to the voluntary abandonment thereof by the Jicarilla and prior to a disruption of their Indian way of life therein sufficient to deprive them of their use and occupation thereof. Dr. Gordon provided relevant survey plats and maps of the area for the relevant years.

The Commission mentioned that grazing was practiced throughout the area, but this had not deterred the Indians from their activities there. The Commission also mentioned that there were two agency locations, at Abiquiu and at Cimarron. These agencies were not reservations, but were merely ration points, locations from which the Indians departed to reach their main subsistence hunting-and-gathering areas.

The Commission mentioned that abortive attempts had been made to provide permanent reservations for the Jicarillas in 1873, 1876, and 1880, but that these attempts had failed, primarily due to the lack of adequate provisions for these Indians on the reservations, which forced them to return to their old way of life in the award area in each instance. In 17 I.C.C. 416–17, the Commission stated that:

> It was not until August 20, 1883, that the old way of life of the Jicarillas in the award area was so disrupted as to deprive them of their use and occupancy of same. This was the date that the military started them on their journey with attendant hardships to Fort Stanton to be joined there with the Mescalero Apaches. Although there was lack of adequate provision for them at Stanton, they stayed on

> there for three years when many escaped to the award area and attempted to engage in their old way of life to a limited extent and in a limited portion of the area.
>
> But the buffalo had disappeared in 1883. This meant that an important reason for their return no longer existed in 1886. During 1884, 1885 and 1886 settlement was developing in the area. The military at Fort Union, located near Santa Fe, taking cognizance of the situation, gave sympathetic understanding and assistance in the light of the attendant circumstances which were brought to the attention of appropriate officials in Washington.

The Commission cited and quoted from a number of decisions that had applied similar facts in their determination of the date of extinguishment of the Jicarilla Apaches' title.

Attorneys for the Tribe filed a motion for rehearing concerning the findings and the opinion of the Commission regarding the land grants. However, the Commission reaffirmed its findings and opinions in this respect on November 9, 1966.

PART III

• • •

VALUATION OF THE AWARD AREA

9

• • •

PRELIMINARIES

After the determination of the date of taking, attorneys for the Tribe employed experts to determine the valuation as of that date. The award area, shown on map 7, was stipulated by the parties to contain 9,218,532 acres; the exterior boundaries were set forth in the Commission's Finding no. 60, 12 I.C.C. 439, 467 (1963).

Generally the area extended to the northeast from its southwest corner near McIntosh, New Mexico (east of the Sandia Mountains near Albuquerque); from east of the Sangre de Cristo Range to the mouth of the Rio Hondo; thence northeasterly along the west bank of the Rio Grande to its point of intersection with the southern boundary of Colorado; thence northeast to Trinidad, Colorado; thence southeast to the northeast corner of New Mexico; thence south along the eastern boundary of New Mexico to its intersection with 30°30' north latitude (near Interstate 40); and thence in a westerly direction to the point of beginning at McIntosh, New Mexico.

The Tribe's principal witness in this phase, Mr. Allen L. McMullen, prepared an extensive appraisal report that was completed in August 1969. The Tribe's other witnesses were Herbert K. Koogle, a consulting engineer; Dr. Leroy Gordon, professor of geography at San Francisco State College (who had testified in previous proceedings); Dahl J. Kirkpatrick, who testified with regard to the value of public lands; and George Ellis, manager of the Bell Ranch in New Mexico, who testified with regard to grazing capacity and quality of lands in eastern New Mexico.

The government's main witnesses were Harley M. McDowell, who testified generally as to the value of the lands in the award area; Ernest Oberbillig, a mining and metallurgical engineer, who testified with regard to the value of mines in the award area; and Mervyn G. Christensen, an appraiser.

Unlike earlier hearings, the hearing on valuation was held before one commissioner, Richard W. Yarborough, on May 14, 15, and 16, 1969. Commissioner Yarborough, after hearing the evidence, filed a report in which he found that the value of the 9,218,532.77 acres in the award area as of August, 1883, was $9,950,000, including minerals and timber, or approximately $1.08 per acre.

Pursuant to rule 28 of the Commission, which provided for a hearing before one commissioner, the attorneys for the Tribe submitted its "Proposed Findings of Fact and Brief" in support of Commissioner Yarborough's report; the government filed a brief objecting to the report. The Commission issued its additional findings of fact and judgment on December 2, 1970 (24 I.C.C. 123), affirming Commissioner Yarborough's award of $1.08 per acre ($9,950,000 total). In the following pages, we review the evidence presented to the Commission by the Tribe and by the government.

Agreement as to Certain Issues

During the hearing and the argument before Commissioner Yarborough, the attorneys for the Tribe and the United States expressly stated that there was no disagreement on many of the basic issues involved in the proceeding, including specifically the following:

1. The highest and best use for the land in the award area at the date of valuation was for grazing.
2. The average carrying capacity for the entire award area was in excess of fourteen animal units per section (640 acres, or 1 square mile) per year. An animal unit is the equivalent of one cow (or one mature steer) or five ewes; yearling cattle are the equivalent of .67 animal units.

3. The cattle-grazing industry was enjoying an economic boom, which reached its peak in 1883.
4. The general nature and quality of the land, such as vegetation, climate, topography, and development by the date of valuation was agreed upon by the parties.
5. The extent of minerals and timber was agreed upon by the parties.
6. Comparative sales were the best evidence of value. The most significant evidence related to the comparative sales of other lands situated either within the award area or near it at about the date of valuation, August 1883.

The essential differences between the parties at the hearing and during the argument concerned the proper identification, description, selection, and treatment of comparative sales, and therefore determination of the value of the land in the award area in the opinion and judgment of the expert witnesses by reference to comparative sales. A secondary issue was the incremental value to be attributed to minerals and timber.

There were ample sales worthy of comparison, and the experts on both sides used many of the same sales, but they reached widely different conclusions as to value. Mr. McDowell testified for the United States that the comparative-value approach indicated a value for the award area of $0.39 per acre. Mr. McMullen testified for the Tribe that it showed a value of more than $1.37 per acre.

The Tribe relied principally on the testimony and report of its appraiser, Allen McMullen, who set forth technical definitions of appraisal methods that said, in part: "Market value is the most probable selling price as of a given period of time," and, "The land being appraised at perfect fee simple title, was free and clear, and possessed unity of ownership, unity of use and contiguity." The importance of the last-mentioned aspects was explained fully in later portions of his report.

Highest and Best Use

Mr. McMullen stated that the highest and best use of the land was for cattle-grazing purposes, ranch settlement, and the development of natural resources. He stated that the land could readily have been sold in 1883 to cattlemen and investors for these purposes. He felt that the great quantity of land, together with the unity of ownership, was compatible with the highest and best use and enhanced the value of the land and its potential.

The award area contains vast acres of the best cattle-grazing land in New Mexico and could even be considered one of the best regions for cattle raising in the Great Plains area, because of its favorable climate and elevation.

A detailed study of the grazing quality of the award area overall indicated a sustained or long-term carrying capacity of 14.8 animal units per section per year; that is, 42.2 acres were required on average to support one animal unit for one year.

Elements of value in addition to grazing use were indicated for the mountainous portion of the award area, due to the value of timber and mineral resources.

Description of the Land

The award area is located in the Great Plains region and extends eastward from the Rocky Mountains. It includes higher plateaus and mesas and portions of the mountainous region to the west. Elevations range from a low of 3,800 feet, in the Canadian River Valley in the southeastern portion of the area, upward to 11,000 feet on the crest of the mountain range in the western portion. Most of the area ranges from 4,000 to 6,000 feet, with some of the higher plateaus at 6,500 feet.

Major rivers or streams include the Rio Grande, Canadian River, Vermejo River, Cimarron Creek, Ocate Creek, Cebolla River, Sapello River, Mora River, Conchas River, Pecos River, Gallinas River, Ute Creek, North Canadian River, and Cimarron River.

The climate of the award area is moderate. Annual precipitation ranges from 14 to 20 inches (the average being from 16 to 18 inches). The mean temperature for July ranges from 84° to 92° and the minimum varies from 54° to 64°. The mean maximum temperature for January ranges from 40° to 52° and the minimum varies from 12° to 20°. The length of the growing season ranges from 120 to 220 days and averages from 160 to 180 days a year.

The principal grasses in the award area were gramma grasses. Brush included chamisa, mountain mahogany, and scrub oak in the higher elevations. Scrub oak, chamisa, and piñon trees were found at 4,000 feet; ponderosa pine and juniper at 7,000 feet; and fir, spruce, and aspen at 8,500 feet and above.

Development in New Mexico by 1883

The first settlement in New Mexico came before 1600, in Santa Fe; by 1870 the population of the territory was 91,874. In 1880 the population was 119,565, and in 1890 it was 153,593 (according to U.S. Census figures). Settlements were distributed principally northward along the Rio Grande Valley; within the award area, they were found along water courses such as the Pecos, Gallinas, Mora, Ocate, Cimarron, Vermejo, and Canadian rivers. Principal settlements in and around the award area were found at Las Vegas, Watrous, Wagon Mound, Springer, Raton, Galisteo, Anton Chico, Mora, Cimarron, and Arroyo Hondo.

There was a high level of activity and homesteading of land in New Mexico both before and after the valuation date. This activity reached a peak in 1883, when 12,847,970 acres of New Mexico land was surveyed, bringing the accumulated total of land surveyed in New Mexico to 36,358,680 acres. By 1891 settlers had paid cash for 640,028 acres in New Mexico, and an additional 622,648 acres of New Mexico land were acquired by individuals through the satisfaction of claim requirements.

The Atchison, Topeka and Santa Fe Railroad, as it approached from the east, reached New Mexico territory in 1878;

by 1883 its rails stretched across the award area into Colorado. Within a few years after that date, it had been extended all the way to California. The railroad greatly improved transportation both to and within the award area, which previously had been restricted to horseback and wagons. The railroad served the flow of western migration into New Mexico, which served to increase the demand for land by settlers.

The suitability of New Mexico for stock raising was recognized from the earliest times. The cattle population of the territory steadily increased after the valuation date (1883) and continued to increase throughout the remainder of the decade. In 1870 there was an estimated 157,000 head; in 1880 the figure had increased to 540,000 head; by 1883 the estimate was 711,000 head. The cattle population continued to increase until 1890, when there were 1,340,000 head of cattle roaming the ranges. It was also noted that the sheep population far exceeded the cattle population.

Development of the Cattle Industry

The cattle industry in the Southwest began around 1850, with early trail drives northward from Texas; the number of cattle driven northward increased notably from 1866 to 1871. In the later years, 700,000 head were herded to the railroad at Abilene, Kansas.

The market had been steady and rising through 1870, but in 1871 there was a sharp decline in prices, which reached bottom in 1873. The industry recovered by 1876, and cattle were being driven west to new ranges blessed with ample grass in New Mexico, Colorado, and Arizona. Then in the early 1880s there came a great boom in the industry, just prior to the valuation date.

The boom brought a market for all the cattle that could be raised. The upward trend in cattle prices for New Mexico beef is evidenced by the following prices quoted in Chicago at the time (see chart 6).

Chart 6

Cattle Prices in 1880s

Year	Number (thousands)	Average Value per Head ($)	Total Value ($1,000)
1880	545	11.10	6,065
1881	567	12.20	6,894
1882	605	13.20	7,998
1883	711	19.50	13,832
1884	812	20.20	16,405
1885	949	18.90	17,940
1886	1065	18.10	19,266

SOURCE: U.S. Department of Agriculture, Livestock on Farms and Ranges 1867-1935

Western Migration and the Cattle Industry

The western migration that began before the introduction of the railroads in the 1870s and that followed them afterward into the early 1880s resulted in the occupation of large portions of Kansas, Nebraska, Texas, and Colorado by settlers. Increases in the populations of Texas and Colorado from 1870 to 1890 were even more marked than those in the New Mexico population for the same periods. Cattle herds were being displaced by the settlers and farmers who were now moving into the neighboring states to the east and north. It was at this time that fencing was introduced to the open range.

The conversion of land in the Midwest from grazing to settlement and farming created a demand for replacement grazing lands in the Southwest and West on the part of alarmed cattlemen.

The response was a westward movement toward the Rockies, into the open spaces where they could enjoy relative freedom of operation on the remaining open range. Cattle grazing in the Great Plains region was steadily compressed into an area extending northward from the panhandle country of Texas and westward to the foothills of the Rockies, bringing with it a substantial demand for land by cattlemen and investors.

The End of the Free Range

The term "free range" was the newcomers' concept. The Indians believed that the land belonged to them and was being taken from them by the intruders; it was not "free." It had been taken forcefully by treaties that ignored proper consideration of the tribes. The Commission, however, adopted the Anglo-American view as revelant to the question of the valuation of the award area.

The windmill came into general use in the prairie region in the period that followed the Civil War. Prior to the invention and general use of the windmill, surface water for stock watering was extremely important to a stock raiser. Lands not reasonably accessible to surface water were frequently controlled by the owners of adjacent lands with surface water. It was common for stock raisers to purchase small amounts of land with surface water and then use large quantities of adjoining land without surface water for the grazing of their cattle.

With the windmill, stock on lands with no access to surface water could be watered through the use of drilled wells. Stock raisers owning lands with surface water could no longer control the uplands, which became increasingly valuable as they were purchased for stock raising.

Barbed wire and the windmill were in general production by 1878. The arrival of the railroad made both innovations available in large quantities to western cattlemen and set the stage for the rapid conversion of the free range into controlled cattle-grazing operations and ranches. Windmills and barbed wire foretold the end of the free range, and cattlemen knew they had to acquire their own grazing land to survive.

Scottish and British Investors

As early as 1879, Scottish financial interests were being solicited by American promoters to purchase and finance newly formed land and cattle companies. Substantial commitments by investors started in 1880, with the formation of the Prairie Cattle Company, Ltd.

From 1879 through 1883, thirty-three companies were registered in Great Britain, with a capital structure of more than $30 million; $20 million was actually paid in and transferred to the United States. The British had as much as $45 million invested in the cattle business in the United States in the 1880s. British and Scottish capital were added to the increasing domestic financial resources already committed to the cattle industry and helped feed the great boom experienced by the cattle industry in that decade.

The Demand for Stock-Raising Land

There was a strong demand by potential purchasers for large areas of grazing land for stock raising at the valuation date. The western migration of settlers resulted in the conversion of rangeland into farms and settlements. The usefulness of remaining range for stock raising was reduced by the interference of the intervening farms; land was needed to replace that loss.

The cattle industry was booming, and prices were increasing. The industry was in a phase of expansion, where additional resources, including land, were being acquired and put to use in cattleraising. Resources were added to the industry by the influx of capital for investment in stock raising from England and France. A significant number of cattle companies were organized as corporations in New Mexico during 1882 and 1883. Cattlemen previously relying on free range for grazing their cattle were forced to acquire lands of their own to maintain their operations.

The great demand for grazing land was confirmed by activity in the sales of grazing land in and near the award area during the period; these sales showed that the demand extended to the award area itself. The demand was further confirmed by inquiries made as to the carrying capacity of the area.

Mr. McMullen testified that one of the most important factors in valuing land that has the highest and best use for grazing, cattle ranching, and stock raising is the carrying capacity of the land.

The Tribe's expert witness with regard to carrying capacity was George Ellis, manager of the Bell Ranch (still one of the largest ranches in northeastern New Mexico). After making his study, Mr. Ellis estimated that the award area held 2,500,000 acres with a carrying capacity of 18 animal units; 2,265,000 acres with a carrying capacity of 16 units; 2,700,000 acres with a carrying capacity of 14 units; 1,000,000 acres with a carrying capacity of 11 units; and 721,000 acres with a carrying capacity of 8 units. His studies showed that the average carrying capacity of the entire award area should be 14.8 units.

Water for Stock Purposes

Many parts of the award area contained streams and other surface waters suitable for stock raising. Water was also accessible throughout the entire area by the utilization of drilled wells and windmills. Because of the windmill, parts of the award area that lacked surface water were not substantially less valuable as grazing lands than the parts providing surface water.

Desirability of the Land

The award area contained some of the best cattle-grazing land in New Mexico and was even considered by many as having some of the best grazinglands in the Great Plains region in general. Moderate temperatures in the summer, with low humidity and cool nights, enabled the cattle to rest and gain weight. Moderate winters and the protection provided by the rolling terrain of hills, plateaus, river breaks, arroyos, and cedar trees resulted in less loss of cattle (especially calves) during the winter months. It was characteristic for winter snows to melt quickly on the southern slopes, thus exposing grass and eliminating the need for special winter feeding. These factors eliminated the need to move cattle to warmer winter pastures, and, together with a good distribution of water, made cattle operations economically more favorable.

Such conditions allowed year-round cattle operations in the award area. Water for stock-raising purposes obtained through the use of windmills was more than adequate, and the carrying capacity of the award area was comparatively good.

The desirability of land in eastern New Mexico was reflected in a letter written in 1882 by Phelps White, a partner in the Prairie Land Cattle Company, Ltd., to Shelton Dowell in Texas:

> We are having fine weather and the grass is coming up for winter feed, our cattle are fattening very fast and the weather will only continue good they will go in the winter in fine fix . . . Remember what cotton did for you some years ago . . . And let it alone . . . There is more money in that grass in one year than you could ever dig out of the farm. My Horses are all in good fix or will be in a short time. Shelt—there is no use talking about the difference in this Country and that [Texas]. I can show you yearlings here that are as large as your four-year-old Steers . . . The only thing about this Country is the scarcity of water . . . If I can ever get Uncle George out here I will try and get him let's try and make tanks off in the river . . . If we can only get water where I want it then there is room here for all the cattle in Texas . . .

10

• • •

VALUATION BY COMPARATIVE SALES

Mr. McMullen's valuation was based in great measure on comparative-sales information. He stated that the most reliable method of valuing land was by reference to the sale of subject lands or similar lands added near the valuation date. "When such sales exist," he said, "the comparative sales basis is the most accurate and should be used."

Numerous sales, both of lands within the exterior boundaries of the award area and of similar lands outside, were made near the valuation date of August 20, 1883. Mr. McMullen prepared a chart showing these sales, making adjustments for various factors (including improvements and fencing, date and price level, location, unusual conditions, and reduction for costs of sale, liquidation, and competition). He stated that these served as an accurate basis for valuing the award area lands at the valuation date (see chart 7).

Comparative Sales Details

The attorneys for the Tribe argued that the acquisition of the XIT Ranch in the Texas panhandle provided an excellent basis for valuing the award area. The XIT lands lay on the eastern boundary of the award area and were comparable to it. Additionally the entire ranch was sold one year before the valuation date, and numerous sales of other large acreages that were part of the ranch were made in 1901 and 1902, when market conditions were still similar to those at the valuation date.

The XIT Ranch was composed of three million acres. Title to the lands was acquired by the Capitol Company in 1888, in an exchange for an agreement made in 1882 to construct the Texas State Capitol in Austin. From 1882 through 1888, the Capitol

Company incurred costs of labor and materials amounting to the equivalent of $1.07 per acre in performing the contract.

Title was not conveyed until completion of construction in 1888, and interest and overhead, which Mr. McMullen conservatively calculated at the equivalent of $0.31 per acre, would properly be added to the materials and labor costs to determine the actual cost of acquiring the ranch. In addition a profit of at least 10 percent, which Mr. McDowell (the government's witness) agreed on cross-examination was proper and should be added, made $1.50 per acre the total cost of acquisition of the XIT land in 1882.

The XIT lands were more valuable than those of the award area because their carrying capacity of 20 animal units per section was greater than the award area's 14.8 units. Mr. McMullen made an adjustment for this greater value and testified that the acquisition of the XIT Ranch strongly supported the $1.08 acre value Commissioner Yarborough reported for the award area.

Mr. McDowell's opinion that the XIT sale indicated a value of $0.50 an acre for the award area was not persuasive, because he erred in using solely the cost of labor and materials of $1.07 an acre for the XIT land value, ignoring completely interest, overhead, and profit. He also erred in stating that the XIT lands were "selected with great care" in order to obtain the most valuable lands, when in fact the XIT purchasers had never seen the lands they were to receive. He also failed completely to explain how he had used the XIT sale to arrive at his valuation of $0.50 an acre for the award area, and there was in fact no logical way he could have done so.

Nine years later, in 1901 and 1902, six sales were made of XIT lands at prices of between $2.00 and $2.04 an acre. The sales of these lands aggregated over one million acres and reliably fixed the value of XIT lands in 1901 and 1902 at approximately $2.00 per acre. The government did not dispute the validity of this sale, but its expert ignored them in valuing the award area.

As stated above, Mr. McMullen adjusted these sales downward to reflect the greater carrying capacity of the XIT lands. It is difficult to determine what weight the Indian Claims Commission gave to the XIT Ranch transactions. The Commission analyzed the transactions in detail, but in the opinion (24 I.C.C. 123) of the Commission, issued December 2, 1970, it indicated on page 129 that:

> The purchase price of the XIT Ranch was done by trading, and the ultimate cost of the land far exceeded the initially agreed price. The transaction has been held not to represent a bona fide sale citing *The Blackfeet and Gros Ventre Tribes of Indians v. United States,* 18 I.C.C., 241, 336 (1967).

Sales of Spanish and Mexican Land-Grant Lands

The Maxwell Land Grant lay within the perimeter of the award area (in the northwest portion), and the award area extended beyond it for large distances on three sides (map 8). However, it was excluded from the award area as a Spanish land grant.

In 1870 most of the grant, totalling 1,679,764 acres, was sold for a price equivalent to $0.80 an acre. Because of the Maxwell Grant's location within the award area, and its similarity to it, its sale provided an excellent basis for valuing the award area.

Actually, however, the award area as a whole had a greater value than that of the Maxwell Grant. Several differences between the two areas were noted by Mr. McMullen. For one thing, the Maxwell Grant had an average carrying capacity of 10.2 animal units compared to 14.8 units for the award area; secondly, the sale of the grant in 1870 came at a time when price levels for stock-raising land were substantially lower than they would have been in 1883; thirdly, the Maxwell Grant had important title defects. The value of the grant lands, moreover, was enhanced by minerals and timber. Considering these factors and the larger size of the award area, it would have commanded a substantially higher price as of the valuation date than the Maxwell Grant did in 1870.

Mr. McDowell, the government appraiser, cited different sales of the grant and argued for a substantially lower value of the grant than did Mr. McMullen. He referred to a sale in 1867 at $0.02 per acre, indicating that it was a valid representation of the value of the grant and of the award area. He did not mention in his report that this sale was between relatives, and was not an arms-length transaction. On cross-examination, however, he admitted this fact; that the sale did not indicate the value of the grant and should not be considered. "This [sale] was only put in for the purpose of showing that the Maxwell Grant was a deed between relatives. This is between relatives, it is not a sale we should consider."

Sangre de Cristo Grant Sale

The sales of portions of the Sangre de Cristo Grant, a land grant located largely within the perimeter of the award area, provided further persuasive support for Commissioner Yarborough's report. Mr. McDowell cited an 1869 sale of 500,000 acres of the northern portion of the grant at a price equal to $2.00 per acre. Mr. McMullen cited an 1871 sale of the 500,000-acre Costillo estate, which constituted the southern portion of the grant, at a price of $1.00 per acre.

The expert appraisers derived radically different values for the award area from these sales. Mr. McDowell determined that the 1869 sale at $2.00 per acre indicated a value for the award area of $.60 an acre, contending that the timber resources, better grazing, and smaller size of the parcel sold motivated the 70 percent discount in valuing the award area. But he was wrong as to timber. His associate, Mr. Mervyn G. Christensen, determined that only one-sixth of the award area's 900,000 acres of timber was merchantable, finding that the merchantable timber had a value in 1883 of $.50 an acre and that the unmerchantable timber had no value at all. If the grant

Chart 7

Comparative Value of Award-Area Land in 1887

Purchases, Date, Location	Acres	Total Valuation ($)	Valuation Per Acre ($)	Indicated Value* ($)
Atlantic & Pacific Railroad, 1884–90 New Mexico, Arizona Cumulative Total	5,316,585	3,835,658	0.72	1.21
Maxwell Grant, 1870 New Mexico, Colorado	1,679,764	1,350,000	0.80	1.21
Sangre de Cristo Grant (Costilla), 1871 New Mexico, Colorado	500,000	500,000	1.00	1.31
Tierra Amarilla Grant, 1883, New Mexico	580,000	800,000	1.38	1.34
Prairie Cattle Company, 1883, New Mexico, Colorado, Texas	139,450	394,644	2.83	1.46
Representative small sales, 1879–83 Colfax County, New Mexico	40,860	105,010	2.57	1.37
Public Domain, 1875–91 New Mexico Cumulative Total	1,270,712	1,588,390	1.25	1.11
XIT Ranch, Acquired 1882 Texas Panhandle				
Net Cost	3,000,000	3,224,593	1.07	
Estimated Invested Cost (No Profit, 1882–88)	3,000,000	4,137,480	1.38	
XIT Ranch Disposal, 1901–2, Sales of Grazing Land	1,028,151	2,056,302	2.00	
Cumulative Total				1.30
Matador Ranch, 1883 Texas Panhandle	374,717	599,547	1.60	1.14
Espuela Ranch, 1883 Texas Panhandle	241,920	515,440	2.13	1.62

Chart 7—*Continued*

Purchases, Date, Location	Acres	Total Valuation ($)	Valuation Per Acre ($)	Indicated Value* ($)
Rocking Chair Ranch, 1883 Texas Panhandle (Sold 1895 @ $0.50/acre)	150,400	188,000	1.25	0.91
Cresswell Ranch, 1885 Texas Panhandle (Sold 1895 @ $1.50/acre)	162,834	325,668	2.00	1.39
Francklyn Cattle Co., 1882 Texas Panhandle (Sold at Foreclosure, 1888, @ $1.20/acre)	637,440	887,654	1.39	1.06
Doyle to Hubbard, 1898 Texas Panhandle	223,622	250,000	1.12	0.89
Childress Company to Swift, 1899 Texas Panhandle	71,553	107,330	1.50	0.99
Gervacio Nolan Grant, 1872, Southern Colorado	48,708	130,000	2.67	1.65
Union Pacific Railroad, 1884, Wyoming and Nebraska	4,321,042	6,517,773	1.51	1.38

* *after adjustments*

SOURCE: Exh. PX1, p. 85

timber were valued on the same basis, the timber value could only be a few cents an acre, even if the entire grant were timber.

Grazing also could not account for the enormous discount made by Mr. McDowell. In fact the award area was more valuable for grazing than the grant. Mr. McDowell admitted that some of the grant range would not support a year-round operation and that there was no other kind of operation in existence at the time of sale. Mr. Ellis, the Tribe's witness, determined that the grant had a carrying capacity of only 8 animal units, just slightly more than half of the award area's carrying capacity of 14.8 units.

Close examination of Mr. McDowell's conclusion showed that there was no reasonable way he could have valued the award area at $0.60 an acre on the basis of this sale. His valuation was unreliable and based on false premises and was undoubtedly disregarded by Commissioner Yarborough.

Mr. McMullen determined that the sale of the Costillo Estate portion of the Sangre de Cristo Grant indicated a value of $1.31 per acre for the award area. This conclusion was reached by adjusting the sale price upward to reflect the higher price values in 1883 than in 1871, the greater carrying capacity of the award area, and the uncertain title to the grant; then adjusting it downward to account for the minerals and timber on the grant and the greater size of the award area. Mr. McMullen's opinion, based on this sale of 500,000 acres located inside the perimeter of the award area, provided further support for the value of approximately $1.08 per acre reported by Commissioner Yarborough.

Sale of the Spur Ranch

The sale of the Spur Ranch in the Texas panhandle also provided convincing support for Commissioner Yarborough and in addition illustrated a technique Mr. McDowell employed to discount comparative sales in determining the value of the award area. Mr. McDowell admitted that the sale of the 242,560-acre ranch in 1883 was made at a price equal to $2.12 an acre. However, he contended that the 242,560 acres controlled another 300,000 acres of free range, so that the actual consideration for the land obtained was only $0.90 per acre.

This contention was wrong. In the first place, the extra acreage was not free range. Mr. McDowell admitted on cross-examination that the acreage was leased at $.06 an acre, a fair rental value for lands worth about $2.00 per acre. Secondly, by 1883 "free range" no longer affected the prices of cattle lands. Mr. McMullen determined that free range had ended in all but the most westerly parts of the plains by 1883, and that this change was evident to everyone at that time. Although some free range might still have been used and controlled in the West, cattlemen could see the imminent end of that situation and would no longer pay a premium for land supposedly controlling "free range." The facts supporting this conclusion were again emphasized by Mr. McMullen:

1. The railroads had made windmills and barbed wire available in large quantities.
2. Lands without surface water could be used for grazing stock and were no longer subject to control by surface water.
3. Barbed wire brought fencing to the range—previously free range became fenced.
4. There was a steady influx of settlers—a certain end of free range.
5. Lands which once controlled free range were no longer sold at a premium.

Even Mr. McDowell admitted these facts:

1. The windmill came into general use in the prairie region following the Civil War.
2. Cattlemen and sheepmen became increasingly dependent upon the windmill for grazing their herds on the uplands.
3. Immigrant farmers began settling and fencing the best valleys and sources of water at the time.
4. Extension of the railroad branches would tend to bring in more settlers.
5. The most successful cattle companies were those which purchased land rather than rely upon range rights.
6. The period of the open range from 1872 to 1882 (wherein ranchers ran cattle on public domain and had little or no fee land) was a transitory period.

Even though Mr. McDowell admitted that the free-range era was over, he still insisted on devaluing the Spur Ranch and other sales using the concept of "free range." This error accounted, in part, for his unrealistically low valuation.

Atlantic and Pacific Lands

Further persuasive evidence in support of Commissioner Yarborough's report was a group of sales involving more than 5,000,000 acres made by the Atlantic and Pacific Railroad (A&P) during a period from 1884 through 1890 that produced an average price of $0.72 per acre. These sales were from checkerboard lands located in western New Mexico and Arizona—alternate section lands acquired from the government in exchange for railroad construction. Although Mr. McDowell cited only the lowest of these sales (one at $0.50 per acre for 1,059,560 acres), neither he nor Mr. Bernard M. Newburg (the government attorney) disputed the validity of the remaining sales, so that the average price per acre of the sales was a much more accurate figure for valuing the A&P lands than the use of just the lowest sale.

The A&P lands were far less valuable than those within the award area. Mr. Tom Cabeen (one of the Tribe's witnesses, who had for many years managed a ranch on A&P lands and was very familiar with the award-area lands) testified that the award-area lands had at least twice the carrying capacity and were twice as valuable as the A&P lands. In addition the greater distances of the A&P lands from cattle markets made them less valuable than the lands in the award area. Also the intervening and alternate sections of public domain made ranching more difficult and detracted from the value of A&P lands.

Mr. McMullen made appropriate upward adjustments to reflect these factors and concluded on this basis that the A&P sales indicated a value of the award area of $1.21 per acre on the valuation date. This figure again provided more support for Commissioner Yarborough's report. Mr. McDowell did not dispute the facts but concluded that the railroad sales indicated a valuation of from $.025 to $0.30 an acre for the award area, a conclusion that bore no relation to reality and was undoubtedly disregarded by Commissioner Yarborough and the full Commission.

Other Sales Cited by Mr. McMullen

Numerous other comparable sales supporting Commissioner Yarborough's report were shown in Mr. McMullen's study. He listed thirteen comparable sales in addition to the ones that were considered in detail above. Mr. Newburg failed to establish any errors or inaccuracies in Mr. McMullen's interpretation of these sales on cross-examination, so that these sales and Mr. McMullen's valuation based on them stood virtually unchallenged. The sales showed values for the award area ranging from $0.90 per acre to $1.65 per acre, with all but four of them indicating values higher than the $1.08 found by Commissioner Yarborough. As a group they established a value of around $1.25 an acre for the award area, strongly supporting Commissioner Yarborough's report.

Sales Cited by Mr. McDowell

Many of the sales cited by Mr. McDowell in his report substantiated Commissioner Yarborough's valuation. In addition to those already discussed, these sales included 100,000 acres sold to the Matador Land and Cattle Company at $1.95 per acre; 750,000 acres in Montana and North Dakota, sold at $1.00 per acre; and over 500,000 acres of the Franklin Land and Cattle Company, sold at $1.32 an acre. There were a number of smaller sales cited, as well.

Many of the sales values on which Mr. McDowell based his opinion of a lower value were determined on cross-examination to be the result of gross errors. For example Mr. McDowell placed great reliance on a purported sale of 574,000 acres of the Tierra Amarilla Grant in 1883 at $0.17 per acre. He called it a "good solid transaction," but on cross-examination, he revised his opinion and admitted that he was suspicious of the sale and had upgraded it (69 Tr. 412):

> **Comment:** I have the deed and it appears to be in all respects good. I have examined the ground thoroughly. I think the land was worth more than that.
>
> **Question:** You weren't suspicious of this transaction because of the low price were you?
>
> **Answer:** I was and for that reason I went to great lengths to research it out, and went on the ground.
>
> **Question:** Nevertheless, you are sure of the Tierra Amarilla Grant [valuation] at $0.17 an acre?
>
> **Answer:** I have the recorded deed for it. I checked the legal description, I checked all the circumstances I could find, I checked the land. I checked everything I could on it. I have even upgraded the sale.
>
> **Question:** Were you not aware that Catron [the purported seller of the grant] continued to own the TA Grant as late as 1901?
>
> **Answer:** No, I wasn't. I did read Dr. Westphal's testimony on this.

The testimony Mr. McDowell admitted to reading was given in Dr. Victor Westphal's deposition—long before Mr. McDowell filed his report. Dr. Westphal stated unequivocally that the "seller" of the grant, Catron, did not sell the grant in 1883, but continued to own it until 1909. Mr. McDowell knew that the sale was not a valid sale and that it should not have been considered.

Mr. McDowell also relied on many other sales that were not valid sales or for other reasons were not proof as to the value of the tracts purportedly sold. His report included a sale of a 3/8 interest in the Pablo Montoya Grant at $1.04 an acre in 1866. He later admitted on cross-examination that a sale of a fractional interest had no probative value, because it did not indicate what a willing purchaser would pay for 100 percent interest in the land and, in fact, there was no title to the grant in 1866; the sale was proven to be a mere speculation.

He listed a report in the *Las Vegas Optic* of a sale priced at $0.17 per acre, but on cross-examination he admitted that he had no idea whatsoever what price per acre the sale actually involved or how much land was sold.

Another sale without probative value was the sale of the Pablo Montoya Grant, which he cited in 1885 at $0.25 an acre. Not only was it the sale of a fractional interest, but it was not even a sale. Mr. McDowell admitted as much on cross-examination (69 Tr. 417):

> **Question:** Let's look at the deed [the deed quoted]. You say yourself that Waddington appears to own the grant as of this date?
>
> **Answer:** Correct.
>
> **Question:** And the deed was from Montoya to Baca?
>
> **Answer:** Right.
>
> **Question:** It was obviously not a sale, was it?
>
> **Answer:** No, but the same consideration may have been put on it. I'm not sure.
>
> **Question:** But it actually doesn't prove a thing, does it?
>
> **Answer:** Not conclusively.

This testimony was typical of Mr. McDowell's approach. He used "sales" that were not sales. He dragged in records for low-priced sales that would support the valuation he wanted to reach, then used them without regard to their validity. It was noted that all of these "sales" were at prices below $0.25 an acre. He claimed that he "factored up" these "sales," but he did not mention this process in his report and often did not even mention their defects. He actually cited a sale between relatives at $0.02 an acre without mentioning a bona fide sale of the same land at $0.80 an acre. His report was essentially disregarded by Commissioner Yarborough and the Indian Claims Commission.

Valuation of Coal, Metallic Minerals, and Timber

The value of the award area was enhanced by the presence of mineral, timber, and coal lands, which were known to exist and were beginning to be developed by 1883 (see chart 8).

Chart 8

Valuation of Timber, Coal and Metallic Minerals in 1887

Resource	Valuation ($)
Timber	
Tribe/McMullen	
583,725 Acres @ $1.43	843,012
Less value of grazing land @ $1.30	(758,192)
Net Value of Timber	75,820
Government/Christensen	
152,000 Acres	76,000
Coal	
Tribe/McMullen	
87,302 Acres	388,475
Government/Oberbillig	
73,600 Acres	245,120
Metallic Mines	
Tribe/McMullen	238,000
Government/Oberbillig	50,000

SOURCE: Exh. PX1, pp. 152–70

Commissioner Yarborough and the Commission did not place a specific value on these resources, but took them into account in reaching their final valuation. The Commission issued its additional findings of fact, opinion, judgment, and order on December 2, 1970, affirming Commissioner Yarborough's valuation as of August 20, 1883, of $9,950,000. The Commission essentially adopted Mr. McMullen's report in reaching a value per acre of $1.08, compared to an appraisal by Mr. McDowell of $0.38 per acre. The Commission stated in its Finding 180 (24 I.C.C. 123, 144), entitled "Market Value," that:

> Based upon the preceding Findings of Fact and the entire record, it is the conclusion of this Commission that, consistent with the highest and best use as grazing lands, the subject area is a unit of 9,218,532.77 acres at a fair market value as of August 20, 1883, of $9,950,000.00, including minerals and timber. Since the United States deprived the Plaintiffs of the lands on August 20, 1883 without payment of any compensation, the Plaintiffs are entitled to a judgment against Defendant in the amount of $9,950,000.00 less allowable gratuitous offsets, if any.

PART IV

• • •

THE FINAL PHASE

11

• • •

COMPROMISE AND SETTLEMENT OF OFFSETS

After the Indian Claims Commission determined that the value of the land taken by the United States from the Tribe for which compensation had not been given was $9,950,000, it was ordered that the Tribe recover from the United States that amount less gratuitous offsets, which would subsequently be allowed. It was further ordered that the case proceed to determination of the offsets, if any were allowable.

The United States, in an amended answer filed in May 1969, requested that it be allowed offsets in the amount of $1,558,779 against the award, for expenditures made by the government for the benefit of the Tribe. In addition it prayed that it be allowed the fair market value of the reservation lands.

After consultation with tribal attorneys, the Jicarilla Apache Tribal Council gave authority to its attorneys to explore a settlement of the offsets. A meeting was then arranged between tribal attorneys and Bernard M. Newburg and Ralph Barney, attorneys for the U.S. Department of Justice to negotiate a settlement and compromise of the offsets.

Prior to the meeting, the claims attorneys had briefed the decisions of the Indian Claims Commission and the Court of Claims on offsets and had made a listing of all expenditures included in the answer of the United States, which were presumably allowable as offsets under the decisions of the Commission. The expenditures included those that were prima facie for the benefit of the United States rather than the Indians; items of expenditure that were too small on an annual basis to be considered as tribal benefits, but were presumably for the benefit of individual Indians; expenditures for the years prior to the date the Indians were placed on the reservation; and other items that had been disallowed by the Indian Claims Commission and were therefore eliminated from the final summary.

The attorneys prepared a "Memorandum of Items Negotiated," which included larger payments to indigent Indians, clothing and subsistence, agricultural equipment, expenditure for livestock, transportation of items that were presumably allowable as offsets, forest management, expenses related to agriculture and cattle raising, and clothing and provisions.

Offsets were discussed at a meeting between the tribal attorneys, Mr. Newburg, and Mr. Barney, on December 16, 1970. It was considered that 50 percent of the items claimed by the government would be a reasonable settlement figure to negotiate.

Mr. Barney stated that items such as clothing and subsistence, care of the tribal herd, and maintenance and conservation of tribal forest lands had been compromised in other cases at 50 percent of the claimed amount. The figure of $500,000 was suggested as a settlement of the cash gratuities. The government had also purchased lands for the Tribe for cash in the amount of $60,570, which would be allowable without any question (see chart 9).

In addition to the cash offsets, the government claimed an offset in an amount equal to the value of the reservation on the date each portion of the reservation was set aside for the Tribe by executive order. The question of the valuation of reservation lands as an offset had not been determined by the Commission. Claimants have argued in the past that reservations set aside should be valued at cost to the government as an offset. The government argued, particularly with regard to public-domain lands, that if the government takes away land occupied by the Indians and the Indians are entitled to compensation for such land at the value as of the date of taking, reservations set aside for the Indians as a partial replacement for the lands should be similarly valued as of the date the reservation is set aside.

The government appraiser, Mr. Harley M. McDowell, valued the 743,618 acres of the reservation at an average of $0.8506 per acre, which amounted to $636,850. Mr. Allen McMullen, in an appraisal completed for the Tribe, valued the reservation lands at $0.3105 an acre for the portion of the reservation lands set aside in 1887, and $0.3503 an acre for the portion set aside in 1907, making a total valuation of $247,416.

The figures considered in reaching the final settlement were based on cash offsets of $500,000, cash purchase of land in the amount of $60,750, and the reservation value at a figure approximating Mr. McMullen's appraised valuation of $247,000 for the 743,618 acres, which made a total of $807,750 for the offsets.

The final settlement for the total land claim of $9,150,000 reflected a deduction of $800,000 in offsets. This was agreed upon by Mr. Barney and Mr. Newburg, subject to the approval of the Jicarilla Tribal Council, the tribal membership, and the U.S. attorney general (acting on behalf of the United States).

A memorandum was prepared for a meeting of the Tribal Council to be held on January 21, 1971, to consider the proposed settlement. We explained the proposal, detailing the offsets claimed by the government, with 50 percent of the claimed amounts that had been agreed upon by the parties as probably allowable. The memo stated in part:

> It is believed by all counsel for the Tribe that the figure of $800,000 is a reasonable compromise on offsets which the government claimed in the amount of $1,558,779 in cash offsets, plus $636,850 for the value of reservation land, for a total claim by the government of $2,189,850.
>
> Regardless of the consideration as to compromise of the offsets, it is clear that litigation of the offset issue would take one and one-half to two years at the minimum to complete without consideration of appeals. Assuming a delay of two years in obtaining a final award, interest on the final settlement amount of $9,150,000 for two years at five per cent would total $915,000, which is in excess of the

Chart 9

Settlement of Offsets

Item	Allowables Claimed ($)	Settlement (50% Basis) ($)
Cash Indigent Indians, 1951	6,558	3,279
Clothing Indigent Indians, 1930–42	2,114	1,057
Clothing	789	394
Subsistence	2,775	1,387
Livestock		
Tribal Herd	10,741	5,370
Provisions	7,556	3,778
Agricultural 1887–1924		
Equipment	18,599	9,299
Clothing	37,337	18,668
Indigent Indians	9,276	4,638
Livestock	1,206	603
Provisions (prior to 1887)	403,413	201,708
Seeds, 1921–24	10,462	5,231
Implements	700	350
Clothing	149	74
Indigent Indians	1,098	549
Provisions	280	140
Transportation, 1884–1900		
Implements	3,341	1,670
Clothing	2,917	1,458
Provisions	5,777	2,888
Forest Management, 1888–1946	220,908	110,454

Continued on next page

Chart 9—*Continued*

Item	Allowables Claimed ($)	Settlement (50% Basis) ($)
Expenses relating to agriculture, cattle raising, implements, etc.	38,050	19,025
Seeds, 1888–1946	8,935	4,467
Sheep industry, 1888-1951	27,300	13,650
Feed and care of livestock	30,766	15,383
Purchase of livestock	1,350	675
Equipment and supplies		
Clothing, 1888–1942	24,329	12,164
Provisions, 1888–1947	40,371	20,350
Transportation of supplies		
Agricultural equipment		
Sch. 67, 1912–50	6,514	3,257
Sch. 83, 1883–1967	5,373	2,686
Clothing		
Sch. 67	1,182	591
Sch. 83	1,961	980
Feed and livestock		
Sch. 67	4,491	2,245
Provisions		
Sch. 67	15,628	7,814
Sch. 83	4,909	2,454
TOTAL	957 ,155	478,736

NOTE: Allowables were included in the General Services Administration report supporting the government offset claims.

SOURCE: Jicarilla Apache Tribal Files

> amount deducted from the valuation award in the compromise settlement. I therefore believe that acceptance of the compromise settlement is in the best interests of the Tribe.

Subsequently on February 12, 1971, Shiro Kashiwa, assistant U.S. attorney general, wrote a letter to Guy Martin, attorney of record for the Tribe, stating that the United States accepted the offer of settlement subject to the following conditions:

1. That the proposed settlement be approved by appropriate resolution of the Jicarilla Apache Tribal Council.
2. That the settlement and resolution of the Jicarilla Apache Tribal Council be approved by the secretary of the interior or his authorized representative.
3. That responsible officials and representative members of the Tribe be present to testify in its behalf at the compromise settlement hearing before the Indian Claims Commission.

Thereafter, in accordance with the resolution of the Tribal Council of January 21, 1971, approving the settlement offer, a general meeting of the Tribe was held to vote on the settlement. The meeting was held on March 16, 1971, and was attended by over 300 adult members of the Tribe, various members of the Bureau of Indian Affairs, and all of the tribal officials and the attorneys.

Counsel gave a detailed presentation at the meeting of the history of the land claim, the length of time expended taking the case to judgment, an assessment of possible delays that could occur if litigation should continue, and the various considerations in favor of the proposed settlement. After a question-and-answer session, a vote was taken; 264 tribal members voted for approval. Not one negative vote was cast.

A resolution was then executed by the president and secretary, which was then properly authenticated by a representative from the Bureau of Indian Affairs, to the effect that the settlement be approved and that it was without prejudice to further prosecution of the accounting claim by the Tribe against the United States.

The attorneys were now authorized to execute a proposed stipulation for entry of final judgment. The compromise settlement was approved by letter from Louis R. Bruce, commissioner of Indian affairs, dated April 1, 1971, to the Tribe's counsel. After setting forth the various steps leading to the settlement, the letter concluded by saying:

> We are satisfied that the meetings of the Jicarilla Apache Tribal Council held on January 21, 1971, and March 16, 1971, and a meeting of the General Council of the Jicarilla Apache Tribe, held on March 16, 1971, were properly called and satisfactorily held. We are further satisfied that the members in attendance at the General Council Meeting reasonably understood the terms of the proposed settlement before voting on it, that those voting were representatives of the Tribe, and the view expressed in the resolution adopted reflect the views of the Tribal membership. The resolutions are hereby approved.
>
> In light of the information that you furnished to us, that submitted by field office, and that obtained from other sources, the proposed settlement of the land claim in Docket No 22-A for a net final judgment of $9,150,000.00 in favor of the Jicarilla Apache Tribe as set out in the proposed "Stipulation for Final Judgment" is hereby approved.

The next step, after the approval of the final settlement, was the entry of a stipulation for final judgment, which was filed before the Commission on April 5, 1971. Then, on April 8, 1971, the Commission held a hearing on the proposed settlement and compromise of the land claim. Counsel for the Tribe made a full statement, setting forth the background of the settlement and the various steps taken to secure the approval of the Tribal Council and tribal members.

The Commission set forth the terms of the final stipulation and made a finding that the joint motion for final judgment, as modified by the terms of the amended stipulation for final judgment, should be granted. The Commission then entered a final award, 25 I.C.C. 248 (1971), which read as follows:

> UPON JOINT MOTION FOR ENTRY OF FINAL JUDGMENT, filed by the parties herein on April 5, 1971, pursuant to a Stipulation for Final Judgment filed with said motion, and subsequently modified by an Amended Stipulation for Final Judgment filed April 20, 1971, the Commission considered the evidence presented, both oral and written, at a hearing called for that purpose on April 8, 1971.
>
> THE COMMISSION, having this day entered additional findings of fact, which are hereby made a part of this order, concludes as a matter of law that the proposed settlement of the plaintiff's land claim is equitable and just to both parties and that final judgment should be entered in accordance with the stipulation as amended.
>
> IT IS THEREFORE ORDERED that the Stipulation for Final Judgment, as amended, is hereby accepted, that the Joint Motion for Entry of Final Judgment is hereby granted, and that the plaintiff shall have and recover from the defendant on its land claim the sum of nine million one hundred fifty thousand dollars ($9,150,000) subject to the terms and provisions set forth in the Stipulation for Final Judgment as amended.
>
> IT IS FURTHER ORDERED that upon motion heretofore filed by the plaintiff on June 27, 1969, that the plaintiff's accounting claim be separated from its land claim, and that the plaintiff's accounting claim be designated as Docket No. 22-K before the Commission.

Appropriation of Judgment Funds and Use of Funds

Congress appropriated $9,150,000 to pay the judgment awarded to the Tribe by the Indian Claims Commission on May 25, 1971 (85 Stat. 40,55). By law the judgment funds could not be used until a plan of use was specifically authorized by act of Congress.

On May 1, 1972, Senator Clinton Anderson of New Mexico submitted a report on behalf of the Committee on Interior and Insular Affairs in support of H.R. 9019, a bill already passed by the House of Representatives, and submitted to the Senate:

> PROVIDING FOR DISPOSITION OF FUNDS APPROPRIATED TO PAY A JUDGMENT IN FAVOR OF THE JICARILLA APACHE TRIBE IN INDIAN CLAIMS COMMITTEE DOCKET NO. 22-A, AND FOR OTHER PURPOSES.

The report recited that an open hearing on the bill had been held by the Indian Affairs Subcommittee, and the committee had ordered the bill reported to the Senate with a do-pass unanimous vote. The report also set forth the purpose of the bill (which was that set forth in the title) and an explanation of the bill (which stated that it would permit money to be used for any purpose requested by the Tribe and approved by the secretary of the interior, that the Tribe had adopted a resolution calling for certain uses, and that the Department of the Interior concurred).

The report of Harrison Loesch, assistant secretary of the interior, followed, outlining the plan for uses of the funds:

1. Community Improvement. $1,500,000 to be invested and the interest drawn upon as needed to provide capital or matching funds for construction of detention and correctional facilities, expansion of the domestic water system, paving of streets, and construction of new sewer systems.

2. Capital Improvement. $3,135,000 to be invested for income and job-producing purposes, including the development of additional lakes to complete the planned recreational program, improvement of a tribal livestock operation, creation of additional game parks, construction of a tribal sawmill, and the acquisition of stocks and bonds.

3. Per Capita Payments. $4,515,000 to be used to make a quarterly per capita payment until each tribal member has received a total of $2,000 ($800 payment and $200 each quarter thereafter).

The report also contained a description of the social and economic conditions of the Tribe; it was approved by Congress on May 16, 1972 (86 Stat. 139).

EPILOGUE

• • •

The two decades since the end of the Jicarilla land claim have been marked by numerous changes for the Tribe, brought about in large part by the lessons learned in the lengthy claim process.

In 1970, the Tribe had filed what became known as the Jicarilla Apache Accounting Case, which dealt with the federal government's mismanagement of the Tribe's timber, grazing, and financial resources. In an unexpected development, rather than resulting in an even more complex and drawn-out litigation, this claim was settled in 1974, for seven million dollars.

Another area of tribal concern was the management of the reservation's oil, natural gas, and coal resources. By 1973 it had become apparent that the Tribe was not being paid royalties based on the true value of the oil and gas produced under leases. Rather than wait for the Department of the Interior to act on the Tribe's behalf, the Tribe's attorneys filed suits in 1974 and 1975 against oil and gas producers that resulted in substantial financial settlements. Even more significant, however, were new arrangements that allowed the Tribe for the first time to enter the oil and gas business as a producer in its own right. These results were important because from the beginning the Tribe had decided to allocate a portion of its natural-resource revenues to a fund for educating its young people. One outgrowth of this litigation was the establishment of the Council of Energy Resource Tribes, founded by tribal President Hubert Velarde and the leaders of twenty-five other tribes from around the country. CERT continues to provide a tribal voice in national energy-policy debates.

In 1976, the Tribe entered into a joint venture with the Palmer Oil Company of Billings, Montana, resulting in seven producing wells; in 1977, it bought out Palmer's interests in these wells, becoming the first tribe in the country to own and operate producing oil and gas wells on its reservation.

Also in 1976, the Tribe decided to institute a tribal severance tax, in addition to negotiated royalties, on oil and gas production; the case was prosecuted by the author from its beginning. After several appeals, the case was heard by the U.S. Supreme Court; it was argued by the author on March 30, 1981. On the last day of the 1981 term, however, Court officials informed the Tribe's attorneys that they should be ready to reargue the case in the 1982 term. The obvious inference was that the Court was deadlocked in a 4–4 tie. Justice Potter Stewart had left the bench. When the case was scheduled to be heard a second time, a new justice would be sitting.

In 1982 the U.S. Supreme Court (with Sandra Day O'Connor as Justice Stewart's replacement) finally ruled, in *Merrion and Bayless, et al. v. Jicarilla Apache Tribe, et al.,* 455 U.S. 130 (1982), that: "The power to tax is an essential attribute of Indian sovereignty because it is a necessary instrument of self-government and territorial management." Today virtually every mineral-producing tribe in the western United States imposes a severance tax on minerals extracted from its lands.

Also in the mid-1970s, the Tribe became involved in a series of water-rights cases concerning the waters of the Navajo River, the source of practically all the reservation's year-round surface flow. Again the Tribe's attorneys preferred to proceed directly in the federal courts, rather than rely on the Department of the Interior to defend its rights, since the department was involved in a dam project that had resulted in a major reduction in flow, as well as damage to the Tribe's municipal waterworks. On October 23, 1992, President George Bush signed P.L. 102–441, a water-settlement contract that awarded the Tribe 40,000 acre feet of water (33,500 acre feet from the Navajo Reservoir or the Navajo River and 6,500 acre feet from the San Juan-Chama project) and $6 million. Lester K. Taylor was responsible for the successful settlement negotiations with the United States and the state of New Mexico. As part of the agreement, the Tribe may subcontract with third parties to supply water for beneficial use off of the reservation.

In the mid-1980s, the Tribe was able to resolve a long-standing concern with its land base. Given the troubled history of the reservation's establishment, it was natural that the Tribe should want to ensure that it had a homeland to which it held title. Through the ground-breaking expedient of offering a tax-exempt tribal bond issue, the Jicarilla Apache Tribe was able, in 1985, to purchase the 55,000-acre Theis Ranch, or Horse Lake Ranch, as the Tribe calls it, and the 24,000-acre El Poso Ranch. The combined price for these two properties was $50 million. As a result of these purchases, the area of the reservation was increased by 10 percent, and the Tribe finally had land it could permanently call its own.

The Tribe is fortunate to possess significant reserves of oil and gas, but these resources are nonrenewable. Timber, on the other hand, will continue to be a revenue-producing resource as long as it is competently managed. At this time the Branch of Forestry of the Bureau of Indian Affairs, Jicarilla Agency, administers these resources, using five-year forest-management plans to arrive at annual allowable cuts. It is almost certain that forestry will take on increased importance as oil and gas production declines in coming years.

Beginning in the 1970s, the Tribe also focused on improving its recreational and tourism programs. By the 1990s, the reservation had become a popular outdoor recreation destination, with outstanding hiking, camping, hunting, and fishing possibilities. And in the mid-1980s, the Tribe financed the construction of a three-million-dollar motel, restaurant, and lounge, which has proven to be an important aspect of its tourism program.

The story of the land claim rests on a rich and varied past, a challenging present, and a promising future. One thing is clear: no matter what the outcome of any particular litigation or tribal enterprise, the Jicarilla Apache people will continue to deal with their circumstances in a spirit of persistence and ingenuity.

NOTES

• • •

1. Citation to all of the authorities on which this account is based would require as many pages as the text. My history of the Jicarilla Apache Land Claim is based primarily on the transcripts of testimony of the experts appearing before the Indian Claims Commission and the unpublished studies made by them in preparation for two hearings before the Commission and one hearing before Commissioner Yarborough alone. Each hearing consumed two weeks of testimony or argument by all attorneys. The government's witnesses disagreed in many instances with the Tribe's witnesses. However, the Commission agreed with the Tribe's contentions in most instances. The historical basis for this account is the testimony and reports of the Tribe's expert witnesses adopted by the Commission, except where otherwise stated. Historians may disagree with the Commission's findings of fact, but for the present purposes, they, together with the statements and reports of the Tribe's expert witnesses, are sufficient authority.

   In transcript citations the first number is the year of the hearing, and the second number is the page number. Transcripts and other official documents of the land claim are in the author's possession and in the National Archives, Washington, D.C.

2. The information obtained through Dr. Thomas's testimony taken on December 1–3, 1958, provided the basis for the accounts of the historical periods.

BIBLIOGRAPHY

• • •

Cohen, Felix S. *Handbook of Federal Indian Law.* Washington, D.C.: U.S. Government Printing Office, 1942.

Cutter, Donald C. "An Inquiry into Indian Land Rights . . . with Particular Reference to the Jicarilla Apache Area of Northeastern New Mexico." In *Apache Indians VI,* American Indian Ethnohistory Series. New York: Garland Publishing, 1974.

Hodge, Frederick W. "Jicarilla." *Handbook of American Indians North of Mexico* 1:631–32. Washington, D.C.: Smithsonian Institution (Bureau of Ethnology, Bulletin 30).

Matson, Daniel S., and A. H. Schroeder, eds. "Cordero's Description of the Apache—1796." *New Mexico Historical Review* 32:335–56.

Reynolds, Mathew G. *Spanish and Mexican Land Laws: New Spain and Mexico.* St. Louis: Buxton and Skinner Stationery Co., 1895.

Rosenthal, H. R. *Their Day in Court: A History of the Indian Claims Commission.* New York: Garland Publishing, 1990.

Terrell, John Uptown. *Land Grab: The Truth about the Winning of the West.* New York: Dial Press, 1972.

Tiller, Veronica E. Velarde. *The Jicarilla Apache Tribe: A History.* Rev. ed. Lincoln and London: University of Nebraska Press, 1992.

U.S. Indian Claims Commission. *Report of the Indian Claims Commission, Sept. 30, 1978.* Washington, D.C.: U.S. Government Printing Office, 1978.

AUTHORITIES

• • •

Cases

Cherokee Nation v. Georgia, 30 U.S. (5 Pet.) 1 (1831)
Elk v. Wilkins, 112 U.S. 94 (1884)
Merrion and Bayless, et al. v. Jicarilla Apache Tribe, et al., 455 U.S. 130 (1982)
Otoe and Missouria Tribe of Indians v. U.S., 131 Ct. Claims 593 (1955)
Tee-Hit-Ton Indians v. U.S., 348 U.S. 272 (1955)
United States v. Santa Fe Pacific R.R. Co., 314 U.S. 339 (1941)

Indian Claims Commission

Blackfeet and Gros Ventre Tribes of Indians v. United States, 18 I.C.C., 241, 336 (1967)
Snake or Paiute Indians v. United States, 4 I.C.C. 571 (1956)
Spokane Tribe of Indians v. United States, 9 I.C.C. 236 (1961)
Jicarilla Apache Tribe v. United States:
- Findings of Fact and Orders:
  - Lands awarded, boundaries: 12 I.C.C. 439 (1963)
  - Date of taking and land grants: 17 I.C.C. 338 (1966)
  - Valuation of award area: 24 I.C.C. 123 (1970)
  - Final judgment: 25 I.C.C. 248 (1971)
- Special Acts of Congress:
  - Appropriation of judgment funds: 85 Stat. 40, 55
  - Disposition of judgment funds: 86 Stat. 139

Treaties

Treaty of Guadalupe Hidalgo, 9 Stat. 922 (1848)

Statutes

9 Stat. 922
10 Stat. 979
12 Stat. 765, 767
43 Stat. 253
48 Stat. 984
49 Stat. 571, 592
60 Stat. 1049
85 Stat. 40, 55
86 Stat. 139
NMSA 1978, secs. 4-6-1 to 4-6-14

Compilations

Recopilación de Leyes de los Reynos de las Indias

INDEX